HIKING VANCOUVER ISLAND

Help Us Keep This Guide Up to Date

Every effort has been made by the authors and editors to make this guide as accurate and useful as possible. However, many things can change after a guide is published—trails are rerouted, regulations change, techniques evolve, facilities come under new management, etc.

We would love to hear from you concerning your experiences with this guide and how you feel it could be improved and kept up to date. While we may not be able to respond to all comments and suggestions, we'll take them to heart and we'll also make certain to share them with the authors. Please send your comments and suggestions to the following address:

> The Globe Pequot Press
> Reader Response/Editorial Department
> P.O. Box 480
> Guilford, CT 06437

Or you may e-mail us at:

> editorial@globe-pequot.com

Thanks for your input, and happy travels!

A FALCON GUIDE®

Hiking
Vancouver
Island

A Guide to Vancouver Island's Greatest Hiking Adventures

Shannon and Lissa Cowan

FALCON®

GUILFORD, CONNECTICUT
HELENA, MONTANA
AN IMPRINT OF THE GLOBE PEQUOT PRESS

A **FALCON** GUIDE ®

Photo credits: Shannon Cowan, Lissa Cowan, Patrick Walshe, and Richard Boyce.

Maps by XNR Productions, Inc. © The Globe Pequot Press

Cowan, Shannon, 1973-
    Hiking Vancouver Island : an atlas of Vancouver Island's greatest hiking adventures / Shannon and Lissa Cowan.
        p. cm. — (A Falcon guide)
    Includes bibliographical references.
    ISBN 0-7627-2350-5
    1. Hiking—British Columbia—Vancouver Island—Guidebooks. 2. Trails—British Columbia—Vancouver Island—Guidebooks. 3. Vancouver Island (B.C.)
    I. Cowan, Lissa. II. Title. III. Series.

GV199.44.C22V363 2003
796.51'09711'2—dc21
                                        2003040806

Manufactured in the United States of America
First Edition/First Printing

Contents

Acknowledgments viii
Introduction ix
  Using This Guide xi
  A Note about British Columbia Parks xii
  Weather and Climate xiv
  Hiking Landscape xv
  Terrestrial and Marine Life xvii
  Aboriginal History xviii
  Map Legend xx

South Island
  1. Galloping Goose Regional Trail 2
  2. Roche Cove Regional Park 9
  3. East Sooke Regional Park (Coast Trail) 13
  4. Thetis Lake 19
  5. Mount Finlayson at Goldstream Provincial Park 22
  6. Cowichan River Footpath 26
  7. Mount Tzouhalem 32
  8. Maple Mountain 35
  9. Cable Bay Nature Trail and Dodd Narrows 39
 10. Piper's Lagoon Park 41
 11. Morrell Nature Sanctuary 44
 12. Newcastle Island Provincial Marine Park 48
 13. Notch Hill 51
    Honorable Mentions
    Sooke Potholes Provincial Park 55
    Kludahk Trail/San Juan Ridge 56
    Ammonite Falls 56

Mid-Island
 14. Englishman River/Morrison Creek 58
 15. Englishman River Falls Provincial Park 61
 16. Little Qualicum Falls Provincial Park 64
 17. Cathedral Grove–MacMillan Provincial Park 66
 18. Mount Arrowsmith (Ridge Access Routes) 68
 19. Mount Arrowsmith (CPR Historic Trail) 72
 20. Della Falls 74
 21. Alone Mountain 80
 22. Puntledge River Trail 83
 23. Boston Ridge/Mount Becher 85
 24. Forbidden Plateau 88

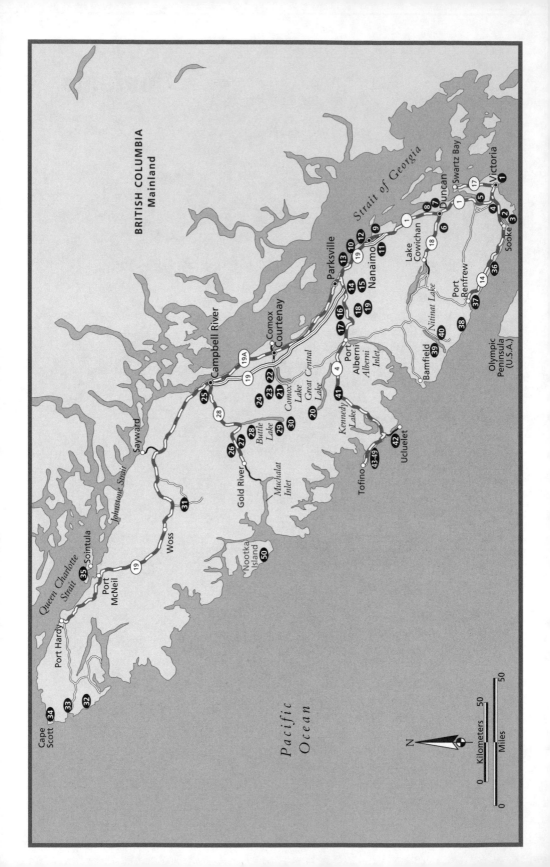

25. Elk Falls Provincial Park 92
26. Crest Mountain 96
27. Elk River Trail/Landslide Lake 100
28. Marble Meadows 105
29. Upper Myra Falls 109
30. Bedwell Lake 112
　　Honorable Mentions
　　Top Bridge Trail 115
　　Lacy Lake 116

North Island
31. Schoen Lake 118
32. Raft Cove 122
33. San Josef Bay/Mount St. Patrick 126
34. Cape Scott 131
35. Beautiful Bay 135
　　Honorable Mentions
　　San Josef Wagon Road 138
　　Ripple Rock 140
　　Mount Cain 140

West Coast
36. Juan de Fuca Marine Trail 142
37. Botanical Beach Provincial Park 148
38. West Coast Trail 151
39. Carmanah Valley 159
40. Walbran Valley 164
41. Clayoquot Valley Witness Trail 168
42. Wild Pacific Trail 172
43. Gold Mine Trail 176
44. South Beach Trail 178
45. Wickaninnish Trail 182
46. Shorepine Bog 184
47. Rainforest Figure Eight 187
48. Spruce Fringe 189
49. Schooner Trail 191
50. Nootka Island 193

The Art of Hiking 203
Appendix 225
　　Hikes Index 225
　　Further Reading 229
　　Clubs and Trail Groups 231
About the Authors 233

Acknowledgments

We'd like to thank the many individuals who have helped us over the course of this book. For providing timely and informative trail reviews: Richard Boyce, John Butterworth, Darrell Frank, Melanie Groves, Val Hignell, Rick McCharles, Dave Rafuse, as well as Dave Forman, Michael Goodhelpson, Hugh MacDonald, Don McLaren, Erv Newcombe, Ron Quilter, Peter Rothermel, Doug Stevens of B.C. Parks, and William Fox of Parks Canada. For assisting us with our many questions: the staff and volunteers at B.C. info centers, logging companies, regional and municipal government offices, B.C. Hydro, B.C. Parks, the Carmanah Forestry Society, and the Wild Pacific Trail Society. For providing timely and thorough trail information: William Cowan Jr., Ken Andrews, and Kathryn Cook.

We'd like to thank Richard Boyce of Island Bound Media Works for providing photographs when our own did not work out, Patrick Walshe for his mapping expertise, as well as editors Scott Adams and Erin Turner for their guidance and support. We'd also like to extend a special thanks to Patrick Walshe, Bridget Walshe, Penny Cowan, Joanne Stone, and William Cowan Jr. for coming along for the hikes, and to William Cowan Sr. for much-needed and frequent transportation.

Introduction

Vancouver Island is a hiker's paradise, but it is also a place of wilderness. Like other pristine environments around the world, vast sections of Vancouver Island are presently feeling the pressures of growth, development, and globalization. The results of these threats include everything from clear-cuts to declining fisheries to the impending extinction of species such as the Vancouver Island marmot. Nowhere are these results more evident then when hiking Vancouver Island's backcountry areas.

Like other hikers, we go out into wild spaces to experience nature and to test our mettle as active human beings. We dislike walking 10 kilometers to view a waterfall surrounded by microwave towers. We are displeased when we have to set up camp next to a backhoe or gasoline tank. The hikes in this book have been chosen for the following reasons to help you avoid those types of encounters:

- They offer a variety of landscapes, vistas, and experiences ranging from alpine wonderlands to wet coast wilderness. Trails moving from low to high elevations often provide the nicest contrasts in wildflowers, forest types, and panoramas.
- They offer special features such as stunning views, dense rain forests, and spectacular waterfalls measured against the hike's worthiness and pleasure.

Don't be fooled by the fragile appearance of the arctic lupine—the entire plant is poisonous.

Take time to enjoy the myriad plant species on Vancouver Island's subalpine trails, such as this edible thistle on Mount Arrowsmith's Saddle Route.

- They avoid (for the most part) the industrial scars of logging, resource extraction, and development, all of which are rampant on sections of Vancouver Island. While these activities exist, we do not feel obliged to visit them on hiking trips.
- They are accessible to most two-wheel-drive vehicles. The exceptions include Marble Meadows, Nootka Island, Newcastle Island, and Della Falls, which are accessible only by boat, floatplane, or ferry.

We write about these areas with the hope that you will treat them with the kind of respect they deserve but rarely receive. We write about them with the hope that you will seek out wild spaces but, at the same time, recognize the need to keep them wild. Both in and out of parks, trail conditions change on a daily basis. The effects of human encroachment and usage leave a large ecological footprint. Please do your best to keep your impact small.

Using This Guide

This guide contains basic instructions and information to help you enjoy more than fifty hikes on Vancouver Island. Some of these hikes are well-trod favorites, while others are little-known paths used mainly by locals. The hikes are organized by area and rated by difficulty. Whether you are a hard-core trekker seeking a multiday backcountry experience or a beginner looking for a level nature walk, you should be physically capable and well prepared before setting out on the trail. It is the responsibility of all hikers to check trail conditions and to research destination information prior to any hiking trip.

Maps
The maps in this guide provide general information on trail features and locations. Use them in conjunction with topographic maps (1:50,000), park brochures, logging road maps, and other information available at tourist information centers across the province. To order tourism information outside British Columbia, contact (800) HELLO–BC (435–5622). To order topographic maps, contact the Centre for Topographic Information, Natural Resources Canada, 615 Booth Street, Room 711, Ottawa, Ontario K1A 0E9; phone (800) 465–6277; Web site maps.nrcan.gc.ca/topographic.html.

Trail Descriptions
When visiting areas both inside and outside parks, contact the sources provided for up-to-date information on trail and road conditions. Unless otherwise noted, trail distances are one-way only and are measured in kilometers. Hiking times are estimated based on light loads, without breaks. Hiking within the recommended season is not a guarantee of desirable weather. In general, trails are official paths with some sort of marking system while routes are unmarked suggestions for further exploration. Routes require map and compass skills and should only be attempted by experienced hikers.

Trail Rating System
The trails in this guide are rated as easy, moderate, or difficult. These ratings depend on the level of skill it takes to complete the trail and how difficult the trail is to follow.

Trailheads

The hikes in this guide may start with an official trailhead kiosk or a lone piece of flagging tape fluttering absently off a tree branch. The level of demarcation is often determined by trail location and jurisdiction. Be on the lookout for all types.

Trail Markers

Most trails in this guide are marked by flagging tape, tree stakes, signposts, rock cairns, or, at the very least, well-defined footpaths. For trails located outside parks, markers may be less official and may change rapidly with time.

Logging Roads

Except for the boat access hikes noted above, all trails in this guide were accessed using two-wheel-drive vehicles. However, road conditions may change without warning. Washouts, landslides, and blowdowns are frequent in British Columbia and occur with some frequency on the private roads providing access to many of these trails. Be sure to check road conditions and access times with the sources given and always carry a spare tire and appropriate maps. Remember that on private roads, logging trucks always have the right-of-way.

A Note about British Columbia Parks

Parks located in British Columbia fall under several categories, including those administered by our national government (national parks), those administered by our provincial government (provincial parks), and those administered by local governments (regional or municipal parks).

Stretching 125 kilometers along the Island's west coast, the Pacific Rim National Park Reserve is the only national park on Vancouver Island. This park contains some of the Island's best-known multiday expeditions, including the spectacular West Coast Trail, as well as shorter day hikes such as those found in and around Long Beach. Year-round camping facilities are available in the Long Beach Unit of the park at Greenpoint Campground.

British Columbia provincial parks protect approximately 12 percent of the province's wild spaces. These parks range from marine areas to urban havens. Most offer some sort of trail system, and many permit overnight camping in wilderness or campground areas. Most parks on Vancouver Island are open year-round, although some campgrounds will be closed in winter and fall.

You'll find some of the largest trees in the world in and around Vancouver Island—like this western red cedar on the Nootka Trail.

▶

Municipal and regional parks exist at various locations throughout Vancouver Island. While these parks do not generally offer overnight camping facilities, most contain trail systems leading to natural points of interest. Municipal and regional parks do not usually require a user fee.

Although each level of government has its own set of rules governing parks in its jurisdiction, the following guidelines apply to most park locations in British Columbia:

- Fires are not permitted in backcountry areas, particularly in areas above the tree line.
- Pets are not permitted in backcountry areas due to difficulties with wildlife.
- Camping is permitted in designated areas only, except in some wilderness parks like Strathcona, Schoen Lake, and Cape Scott.
- Most parks charge a user fee for overnight camping. Paying this fee ensures that our parks will continue to offer safe and pristine wilderness experiences.

Trail information is constantly being updated by the appropriate agency or organization. Trail conditions and trailhead access changes on an ongoing basis. Use the contact information given at the end of each listing to find out more about your hike. Some parks also offer programming for children and adults. For more information about fees and services, or to make reservations, contact:

Parks Canada: (800) 748–7275.

B.C. Parks General Information: (250) 387–4550.

B.C. Parks Reservation Line (March 1–September 15): (800) 689–9025 (throughout Canada and the United States) or (604) 689–9025 (in Vancouver).

Weather and Climate

Vancouver Island is known for its temperate climate. There is a saying that the Island is "Canada's California." While this might be a bit of a stretch, it isn't exceptional to see golfers teeing off in January while skiers check out the deep powder on local mountains. Because Vancouver Island is along the Pacific coast of North America, the warm winds and currents of the Pacific greatly influence its climate. These warm winds keep the climate mild so the Island seldom sees snow in winter at lower elevations.

Unfortunately, mild temperatures mean more rain. The moisture-laden ocean air first hits the westerly mountains, dumping huge quantities of rain in some areas. While this may seem like a deterrent, these rains are responsible for creating and sustaining Vancouver Island's spectacular rain forests, home to some of the biggest trees in the world. The most important thing for hikers to remember is that most rainfall occurs during the winter months, with wide variations across the Island. When checking weather conditions it's a good idea to always check for specific areas. Visit Environment Canada's Web site (www.weatheroffice.ec.gc.ca) for up-to-date information about Island weather conditions.

Southeast coastal areas of Vancouver Island are mostly dry. Mountain ranges are cooler throughout the year and receive snowfall instead of rain. The spring snowpack can be as deep as 5 meters, lingering well into August. Although most mountain hikes involve snow, some of the most spectacular views on Vancouver Island are found on mountaintops. At higher altitudes you'll encounter some pretty extreme conditions. Proper preparation and the right gear are the keys to staying comfortable. When planning an alpine or subalpine hike, remember that snow requires extra equipment such as an ice ax, gaiters, and appropriate footwear. Vancouver Island's west coast is a favorite hot spot for surfers. Because this side of the Island is exposed to the westerly winds blowing off the warmer Pacific Ocean, it is windier than other areas.

The coldest temperatures come to Vancouver Island in January. If the weather blows up from the south, Islanders can expect above freezing temps in the 5 to 8 degrees C range in the day, and down around freezing at night. Sometimes the Island is hit with arctic outflows that drift down the mainland mountains and funnel out over the lower mainland and over to the Island. As these air masses cross the Strait of Georgia, they pick up moisture and dump snow on the Island.

Here are some climate averages for Vancouver Island:

- Annual rainfall: 68.5 cm per year
- Summer temperatures: 18–32 degrees C
- Winter temperatures: 5–16 degrees C

Hiking Landscape

Measuring 450 kilometers long and 100 kilometers at its widest point, Vancouver Island is the largest island on the west coast of North America. Vast stretches of ocean beach, glacial mountains, and dense rain forests top off this rich natural landscape, promising hikers some of the most awe-inspiring and diverse hiking trails in the world.

The Island's highest mountain, the Golden Hinde, rises 2,200 meters and is located smack dab in the middle of Vancouver Island. A handful of the highest summits reach 2,100 meters and climb from deep valleys at a scant 225 meters. The Island's alpine ridges measure roughly 1,200 meters. When crossing from ridgetop to ridgetop across the valleys, the ascent for hikers can be quite a climb. The Island's alpine heights are open, sprinkled with heather, mosses, sedges, and other low-growing plants. In springtime, in subalpine meadows, a rich assortment of flowers such as edible thistle and various species of aster, daisy, lupine, and lily make for a regular botanical garden.

The Island's forests vary in age from second growth to mature stands

with multiple canopies. Although mixed forests exist, conifers such as Douglas fir and western hemlock dominate most of the Island. In these cathedral-like forests, hanging lichens, mosses, and ferns abound along with salal, skunk cabbage, huckleberry, and wild ginger. The forest and alpine regions are home to countless varieties of mushrooms and fungus. Although there is no poison ivy on the Island, the indigenous devil's-club takes its place quite nicely. Characterized by its 2-meter spiny stalks and broad leaves, this plant is usually found growing in valley floors or creekbeds. The spines can produce nasty rashes and even infections. Needless to say, cross stands of devil's-club with care.

Before setting out, check that your car jack kit is complete and the air pressure in your spare tire is good. It is preferable for hikers to carry two spare tires, because logging roads often bring unpleasant surprises. Researching current logging road conditions is also important. Many valleys were logged and deserted years ago, and a road marked on a map is no indication of its driving condition. It is worth noting that most rental car companies' insurance policies are null and void when traveling on gravel roads.

Terrestrial and Marine Life

On land and off its rocky shores, Vancouver Island offers hikers an awesome diversity of terrestrial and marine life. Due to its separation from the rest of mainland British Columbia by the Strait of Georgia, the Island has developed a unique blend of wildlife. The endangered Vancouver Island marmot is just one example. Trails through temperate rain forests, mountainous regions, and valleys are perfect spots for amateur bird-watchers to view a variety of local songbirds. Paths that hug the shoreline allow hikers to catch a glimpse of many shorebirds and raptors, including cormorants, ducks, herons, bald eagles, ospreys, and kingfishers. Larger animals include black bear, cougar, wolf, black-tailed deer, and Roosevelt elk. Sasquatch have also been known to frequent areas near Strathcona Park.

In the waters surrounding Vancouver Island—especially those off the Island's west coast—explorers may catch sight of a pod of orcas or gray whales slapping their tails on the water's surface or spouting sea mist. Often seals, sea lions, and otters sunbathe on the Island's craggy shoreline, while tidal pools provide hikers with the chance to view anemones, sea stars, and crabs. In many coastal areas shellfish, including crab, oysters, and clams, litter the beaches. Interior lakes and streams, many of them stocked, are home to large populations of trout.

Because cougars have been known to attack domestic pets, it is better to leave your four-legged friend at home when hiking in wilderness areas.

◀ *A stone's throw from the City of Nanaimo, Sandstone Beach on Newcastle Island is one of many breathtaking seascapes in the Vancouver area.*

Keep in mind that local hikers very rarely see cougars. Problems with bears are also infrequent. The Island's forest provides them with an abundance of natural food, and they rarely have cause to approach people. This situation will only remain, however, if backcountry travelers take precautions not to attract them in the first place. There is no foolproof way to scare off a bear or a cougar, but there are ways to avoid encounters. For more information, see the Art of Hiking section at the end of this book. In general, Island wildlife is shy and elusive. If you are fortunate to have a sighting, treasure the moment and remember that you are a visitor in their domain.

Aboriginal History

For thousands of years aboriginal peoples have lived on Vancouver Island. If you stare up at a towering red cedar while hiking West Coast Trail or visit Goldstream Provincial Park during the salmon run in November, you might imagine the life of aboriginal peoples on the Island prior to European arrival.

Tied to the natural world, these ancient peoples fished for salmon and trout in the countless rivers, lakes, and in the Pacific Ocean. In forests they hunted bear and deer, collecting a rich variety of plants to be used for preparing traditional foods. Today many local fruits used by the Island's first peoples such as salal, blackberry, salmonberry, wild strawberry, gooseberry, and currant may be spotted (and sampled) while hiking through lush temperate rain forests.

The natural environment in which the aboriginal peoples lived formed the backbone of their customs and traditions. Plant roots were gathered for medicines, while bark, stems, and leaves were used for making mats, baskets, and bags. These peoples relied heavily on the red cedar for both practical and spiritual purposes. The tree's bark served for shelter and clothing while the wood was carved into canoes, totem poles, and ceremonial items. In areas where the B.C. coastal rain forest has been protected, you might be lucky enough to catch a glimpse of the past in the form of what's known as a culturally modified tree. Still practiced today by a handful of artist mask makers, the task involves cutting or burning the center of the red cedar, leaving the greater part of the tree intact to grow back.

When hiking on Vancouver Island, you may notice several place names such as Cowichan, Songhees, and Sooke that can be attributed to the Island's first inhabitants. Also evident in many Island areas are English- and Spanish-sounding names such as Vancouver, Barkley, Narvaez, Quadra, and Quimper. These explorers and navigators came following Captain James Cook's arrival on Vancouver Island in 1778. The Gulf Islands of Quadra, Cortes, Valdes, and others also carry the names of early Spanish explorers.

With the influx of Europeans came the large-scale exploitation of the Island's natural resources. In 1842 the Hudson's Bay Company built a fort on the southern tip of the Island. Named for Queen Victoria, the fort became what is now known as Victoria. This is the Island's largest city and a throwback to the English colonial era of high teas and croquet.

In 1884 the dominion government outlawed aboriginal potlatch ceremonies. They seized ceremonial dress, including masks, rattles, robes, and coppers. These ceremonies, which mark important occasions such as births, marriages, deaths, or the transfer of names, went underground following this ruling.

Following the Supreme Court decision in 1973 and Canada's decision to negotiate settlement of outstanding aboriginal land claims, treaty negotiations between Canada and the Nisga'a began in 1976. British Columbia joined negotiations in 1990, and an agreement in principle was signed in March 1996. The two senior governments and First Nations representatives of British Columbia appointed the B.C. Treaty Commission in 1993 to facilitate negotiations of treaties with other First Nations in the province. By 1996 most coastal tribes had filed Statements of Intent to negotiate treaties under the Treaty Commission process. Because most of the province is still under treaty negotiations, the story is not over. Where trails in this guidebook cross First Nations land, we have made every attempt to include contact information. Develop a good hiker's reflex by getting permission before setting foot on a trail.

Map Legend

═══════	Limited access highway
═══⟨14⟩═══	Provincial highway
──────────	Other road/route
──────────	Gravel road
═ ═ ═ ═ ═	Unimproved road
▬▬▬▬▬▬	Featured trail
─ ─ ─ ─ ─	Other trail/route
··············	Low tide route
┼┼┼┼┼┼┼	Railroad
─·─·─	Pipeline
─•──•─	Powerline
⌐ ¯ ˥ Parks	Parks
⌐ I.R. ˥	First Nations land
▲	Campground or site
⫽	Falls
•–•	Gate
⋈	Bridge
◙	Overlook/viewpoint
🅿	Parking
▲	Peak
▪	Point of interest
START	Trailhead

South
Island

Telling stories has always been part of the experience of southern Vancouver Island inhabitants. In ancient times Central Coast Salish people believed that animals, trees, rocks, and places were part of their families. Stories etched into rocks in what is now known as East Sooke Regional Park by these first people are testimony to a culture in which tales of ancestors, human and nonhuman, dominated the day. Once a colonial outpost, Victoria, the province's capital city, continues to tell stories about its much-younger 150-year history. These living history lessons are visible throughout the city in nineteenth-century-style lamp-posts, horse-drawn carriages, countless museums, double-decker buses, and restored post-Victorian homes. The quaint town of Chemainus recounts its town's history through a series of vibrant outdoor murals.

In addition to Victoria, southern Vancouver Island includes places such as Duncan, Lake Cowichan, Ladysmith, Nanaimo, and Chemainus. Located northwest of the province's capital, these towns became strong largely from harvest and timber production. They've retained their unique historical character all the while evolving as older industries give way to new ones such as ecotourism, cultural activities, and marine, forestry, and agriculture research.

Located across the Juan de Fuca Strait from Port Angeles and Olympic National Park, Victoria is popular among tourists who flock to Butchart Gardens. Often visitors don't realize that, just outside the city, lies an abundance of top-rate hiking spots unique in natural beauty, wildlife, and adventure. Observing marine life at Becher Bay, hiking the Cowichan River Footpath, experiencing the Trans Canada Trail, or cycling through Victoria and along the Saanich Peninsula on the Galloping Goose Regional Trail, there is no shortage of stunning scenery and awesome hiking in this area. Craggy coves, crystal-clear beaches, waterfalls, summits, towering Douglas fir, Garry oak forests, and arbutus groves are just a few South Island delights.

The 1858 discovery of gold in the Fraser River transformed Victoria. Miners and adventurers donning pans and spades set up tents around the fort that was established by the Hudson's Bay Company to advance the fur trade. But yesterday's adventurers are today's hikers. Outfitted with backpacks, maps, and rain gear, these rugged-minded and environmentally conscious individuals may be spotted grabbing a coffee (a west coast custom) in a sunny Victoria cafe before leaving the city for greener, wilder places.

Galloping Goose Regional Trail

The Galloping Goose includes a sampling of urban and rural vistas. The trail—named for a local 1920s railway car—cuts through British Columbia's capital city of Victoria. Highlights include wildflower fields, wall murals, rocky outcrops, graffiti, Garry oak, ocean views, wetlands, lakes, and streams. Because this trail encompasses such a wide variety of city and nature, its highlights include everything from breathtaking ravines and country fields to inspiring murals and creek restoration projects. Given the trail's unique railway past, it is different from most other hiking trails in that it includes lengthy trestle bridges and vistas formerly seen through a train window.

Distance: 46 kilometers to Todd Trestle (Sooke Potholes Provincial Park). The trail extends 55 kilometers to Leechtown.

Approximate hiking time: When exploring the Galloping Goose Regional Trail by foot, you may decide to visit one or two specific sections rather than walking the whole thing. This is because the trail breaks up at several intervals and covers a wide range of features and territories. Many people opt to cycle the Galloping Goose, because the path—which follows what used to be a rail line—is wide and level most of the way and can be completed in two to three days. Because the trail either borders or cuts through countless regional and provincial parks such as Roche Cove, East Sooke, Thetis Lake, and Sooke Potholes, you may choose to extend your trip to include additional hiking excursions.

Difficulty: Easy to moderate.

Type of hike: Dubbed "The Goose" by locals, this six-year-old route can be enjoyed on foot, in-line skates, horseback, or bicycle. The trail spans the distance from Swartz Bay to Sidney in the north, then continues on to Saanich, Victoria, Esquimalt, and View Royal to the east, until finally heading west to Colwood, Metchosin, and Sooke where it completes its long journey at Leechtown. Though there is ample signage and many municipal crosswalks over busy streets and highways, some spots lack proper signage for vehicles and can be hazardous to trail users. For the most part, South Island residents are courteous. However, use caution when crossing roads. Always yield to car traffic and walk your bike across all intersecting roads. Trail etiquette suggests that you call out to trail users when passing on the left.

Elevation gain: No significant elevation gain.

Best season: Year-round.

Land status: Regional trail.

Finding the trailhead: Before setting out, pick up a Galloping Goose trail map from a local tourist bureau. If you have the computer software Acrobat Reader by Adobe, the *Galloping Goose Regional Trail Guide* is available through the Capital Regional District (CRD) Parks Web site at www.crd.bc.ca/parks. The trail can be picked up at several access points along its circuit, depending on which trail features you wish to explore. Parking areas are located along the way at Atkins Avenue in View Royal, Aldeane Avenue in Colwood, near Luxton Fairgrounds on Sooke Road in Luxton, Rocky Road Point in Metchosin, and Roche Cove Regional Park in East Sooke. At most of these access points, there are public toilets and small day-use picnic areas. The Goose officially starts at the Johnson Street Bridge in downtown Victoria. An information kiosk on the west side of the

Galloping Goose Regional Trail

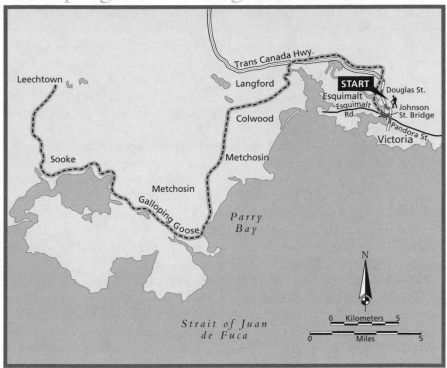

bridge is there to orient visitors. The markers along the trail clock distance in kilometers from this point.

If you choose to begin the Goose at the Selkirk Trestle, drive over the Johnson Street Bridge to the north side. Follow Skinner Road and turn right onto Tyee Road, where you'll find free parking by the side of the road to the right. Walk to the end of Tyee Road to meet the Goose leading into a forested area (watch for signs). A cafe and bike rental shop are on your left before you arrive at the trailhead.

The hike: **Selkirk Trestle to Switch Bridge (about 2 km):** Located northwest from Victoria's inner harbor, the Selkirk Trestle is made of fir and hemlock and measures 300 meters long. This immense bridge is wide enough to withstand all manner of in-line skaters, strollers, cyclists, and joggers. When crossing the trestle, watch for kayakers and rowers on the Selkirk Water below. In this urban section, prepare to cross several city roads as the Goose sweeps past the backs of old factory buildings (graffiti included!) and a few houses with country gardens. The trail will take you underneath two bridges: Burnside Road East Bridge and Gorge Road East Bridge. On the latter, a vibrant mural is painted on the underside. On this first leg of the trail, the semiurban naturescape consists of mostly willow, maple, and some poplar.

Switch Bridge to Swan Lake Christmas Hill Nature Sanctuary (about 1.5 km): The Goose meets a fork just past the Switch Bridge (100 meters) that crosses over the Trans Canada Highway. To the right (northeast) is an offshoot that passes by Swan Lake Christmas Hill Nature Sanctuary, which encompasses fifty-eight hectares of marshy lowlands and nature trails. This northeast line of the Goose is part of the Lochside Trail that continues to Sidney. Take note that bikes are not allowed within the protected area. Bike racks are located near interpretive panels and within close range of the sanctuary, which is abundant with wild flora including Garry oak.

Switch Bridge to Thetis Lake Regional Park (about 6 km): Returning to the fork (about 1.5 kilometers from the nature sanctuary), you can then take the left fork (west), which eventually leads to the communities of View Royal, Langford, and Colwood. The paved section of the trail turns to gravel about 6 kilometers from the Switch Bridge. Heading west, the Goose parallels the Trans Canada Highway for about 6 kilometers until it nears a vehicle access point at Thetis Lake Regional Park. This park, known for its twin lakes, is a great spot to picnic and swim on a hot summer day.

Thetis Lake Regional Park to Glen Lake (about 6 km): Continuing on past Thetis Lake Regional Park, the Goose descends southwest toward the community of Colwood. At Atkins Avenue (approximately 2 kilometers from the Thetis Lake parking lot) the trail follows an old railbed and goes from being paved to a more rugged, though still level, path. During this leg the Goose will intersect with Atkins Avenue and Sooke Road three times. The trail passes by the Juan de Fuca Plaza and the Colwood Plaza, crosses Highway 14 (Sooke Road), and meets up with Aldeane Avenue. History buffs with some time to spare might wish to take a brief detour (more than 1 kilometer) along Ocean Boulevard (at Colwood Plaza) to visit Fort Rodd Hill National Historic Park and Fisgard Lighthouse. These historic sites are located southeast of the Goose. At Aldeane Avenue and Sooke Road is a vehicle access point. Here you'll notice the entrance to Royal Roads University, which is also the location of Hatley Castle. The trail crosses over Millstream Road and hectic Jacklin Road prior to arriving at Glen Lake.

Glen Lake to Rocky Point Road (about 13 km): Just past Glen Lake where the Goose intersects Highway 14 (Sooke Road) is another vehicle access point. The trail then passes Luxton Fairgrounds on the right and begins flying south toward the District of Metchosin, one of the first Vancouver Island settlements. The Goose parallels Happy Valley Road for about 7 kilometers before meeting Rocky Point Road to the west. Here you'll glide (if on a bike) past quaint farms where cows graze in meadows near clusters of yellow flowering broom (in spring). This is a pleasant spot to stop and admire the scenery. Perch on a rock along the trail edged with wildflowers and comb the skies for bald eagles or turkey vultures.

Rocky Point Road to Roche Cove (about 5 km): Following the junction of Rocky Point Road and Kangaroo Road, the trail parallels Rocky Point Road

This giant mural on the underside of a bridge enhances the urban section of the Galloping Goose Regional Trail.

for about 3 kilometers until it crosses this road a second time and arrives at a vehicle access point located at Matheson Lake Regional Park. In summertime this freshwater lake is rampant with paddlers, anglers, and swimmers and comprises a 3-kilometer hiking loop. Here the trail is carved into the Sooke hills with glimpses of Matheson Lake. Watch for bald eagles or walk down to the lake 20 meters below and leave your bike behind. On this leg of the trail, you'll start to notice more examples of old-growth Douglas fir, hemlock, and western red cedar. Around Matheson Lake and Roche Cove, the forest becomes denser while sword ferns, salal, and local berry varieties such as huckleberry and salmonberry border the trail.

Many people who hike or bike the Goose begin their journey at Roche Cove Regional Park. This is because the rustic atmosphere to the east combined with the

untamed natural beauty of second-growth forests and lakeside, river, and seaside vistas to the west is pleasant to behold and well within reach during a day trip. Another vehicle access point that is just south of Roche Cove is located at Malloch Road along Rocky Point Road. From these two access points, you can travel to an assortment of regional parks that are popular for hiking, swimming, and picnicking such as Witty's Lagoon, Devonian Park, Matheson Lake, and Roche Cove.

Roche Cove Regional Park is a particularly interesting spot to explore. This park offers hikers up to 7 kilometers of trails along with a few highlights such as the cove and meandering Matheson Creek. Stop for a snack at the sheltered Roche Cove before picking up the Goose once again on its way to Sooke Basin.

Roche Cove to Sooke River Valley (about 6 km): The trail crosses over Gillespie Road and borders the Sooke Basin heading north to Milnes Landing. The Sooke River flows southwest from Sooke Lake and empties into this body of water. Sooke, which is the name of this district, acquired its title from the T'Sou-ke native band, which is also the name of a species of stickleback fish that was at one time plentiful in the Sooke Basin. It is here, where the trail follows the water, that trail users get a real sense of what it must have been like to ride the old passenger train between Victoria and Sooke. The trail is carved into the rocky headlands with barely any land between the wide path and the water below. Along the trail's edge, on the side of the forest, are benches dedicated to locals who spent time enjoying these spectacular vistas. Looking out at Sooke Basin, you might be lucky enough to view buffleheads or Barrow's golden eyes riding the waves.

Here the Goose nears Hutchinson Cove, where it then dips down and crosses a bridge over Veitch Creek that flows into the basin. This is a lovely little spot to meditate and admire the spectacle and sounds of the water below. Before once again meeting up with Highway 14 (Sooke Road), the trail nears Cooper Cove ahead of the Sooke River Valley.

Sooke River Valley to Charters Creek Trestle (about 4 km): As the Goose approaches the mouth of the Sooke River, it heads north and ascends the Sooke River Canyon to Charters Trestle at Charters Creek.

Charters (Creek) Trestle to Leechtown: About 2 kilometers past Charters Trestle is another wooden and iron trestle called Todd Trestle. Located at Todd Creek, this trestle was also part of the old railway and has since been updated to safely accommodate hikers, horses, strollers, and bicycles. Situated between the two trestles is Sooke Potholes Provincial Park. Here you'll see falls carving a history of bizarre sculptures out of the surrounding limestone cliffs and rock faces. If you're starting your journey on the Goose at this entrance point, you can drive into the park. The only drawback is that vehicles must pay a daily fee to use the year-round access route at this privately owned campground. For more information, contact Deertrail Campgrounds Adventure Gateway at (250) 382–3337. The Goose cuts through the campground just past Rippling Rock Beach and a gravel pit to your left. You'll see caution signs for park vehicles and a sign designating the trail. A parking lot for users of the Goose is located just past this point.

The last 12-kilometer stretch of the Goose is level and straight and doesn't hold a candle to the fantastic scenery of the other sections. After the Todd Trestle, the trail returns to the forest on its way to Leechtown. It follows the Sooke River all the way along until it reaches its destination.

Leechtown had its heyday when prospectors struck gold in the area in 1868. This last section of the trail is purported to be wilder and more isolated, so mind the bears and cougars. Weeds and wildflowers have overtaken the abandoned mining town, leaving few visible reminders of the original settlement. It's a nice quiet spot to relax at the end of your long trek and to commend yourself on a job well done.

Key points (km)

0.0   The Goose officially starts at the Johnson Street Bridge. Markers along the side of the trail clock distance in kilometers from this point.

2.0   Begin the trail at the Selkirk Trestle.

3.0   Just past the Switch Bridge is a fork with options to follow the trail to View Royal in the direction of Thetis Lake Regional Park. Another option is to head to the right (east) to view the Swan Lake Christmas Hill Nature Sanctuary.

4.0   The Goose crosses over the Switch Bridge heading northwest in the direction of View Royal.

5.0   The trail reaches Swan Lake Nature Sanctuary.

7.0   The trail parallels Burnside Road West.

8.0   The trail crosses over the Trans Canada Highway and parallels the highway for about 3 kilometers.

10.0   The trail reaches Thetis Lake Regional Park. This is a vehicle access point for the Goose. The park includes seven short hiking trails making up 13 kilometers in total. During the summer months people flock to this clear-water lake to swim.

12.0   The trail crosses Atkins Road and parallels the road for a brief moment before veering left (south) past the Juan de Fuca Plaza and crossing over the Old Island Highway.

13.0 The trail crosses Sooke Road.

14.0 The trail crosses Sooke Road a second time, this time nearing Royal Roads University. This area is known as Colwood. At this junction is a vehicle access point for the Goose. The trail crosses the road and continues along Aldeane Avenue past Colwood Lake to the right.

17.0 The trail crosses Jacklin Road and meets Glen Cove Park and Glen Lake to the right. Just past Glen Lake (about 0.6 kilometer) is another vehicle access point located on Sooke Road, not far from the Luxton Fairgrounds.

18.0 After meeting Sooke Road again, the Goose wanders to the left, heading southwest along Happy Valley Road for about 3 kilometers. Here it crosses several secondary streets before entering the District of Metchosin.

23.0 Crossing Lindholm Road, the Goose flies southeasterly.

25.0 The trail comes to Rocky Point Road.

29.0 After crossing Rocky Road Point a second time, the Goose enters a parking area that is a vehicle access point for hikers and cyclists of the trail.

32.0 The trail borders the lake. Matheson Lake is a popular spot for swimming, fishing, and paddling on hot summer days.

33.0 The trail arrives at Matheson Lake Regional Park. This green space consists of 162 hectares of well-traveled 3-kilometer hiking and walking trail loops around Matheson Park.

34.0 The trail enters Roche Cove Regional Park and follows Matheson Creek. Here is another vehicle access point for the Goose. There are public toilets at this park, which offers 7 kilometers of park trails. A few of these trails border Matheson Creek and lead to the serene but windy Roche Cove.

38.0 The Goose reaches Hutchinson Cove, which is part of the Sooke Basin. Sooke Road is to your right.

40.0 The trail borders Sooke Road heading west. This area is called Saseenos.

43.0 Heading north, the Goose reaches a vehicle access point with public toilets. From this point it will follow one of the last legs of the journey along Sooke River to the Todd Trestle.

45.0 The Goose enters Sooke Potholes Provincial Park, where adjacent riverside campsites are available on privately owned land.

46.0 The trail arrives at Todd Trestle, which is situated at the junction of Todd Creek and Sooke River.

   Option: Continue on the Goose, which parallels the Sooke River to Leechtown.

55.0 The trail arrives at Leechtown, an abandoned mining village that has long since vanished. In its place are quiet woods with opportunities to view wildlife.

Hike Information

Trail Contact
Capital Regional District (CRD) Parks, 490 Atkins Avenue, Victoria, BC V9B 2Z8; phone (250) 478–3344; fax: (250) 478–5416; recorded information (250) 474–PARK; Web site www.crd.bc.ca/parks; e-mail crdparks@crd.bc.ca.

Fees/Permits
No fees or permits required.

Local Information
Greater Victoria Cycling Coalition, 1056 A North Park Street, Victoria, BC V8T 1C6; phone (250) 480–5155; e-mail gvcc@gvcc.bc.ca.

Bike Rentals
Note that several urban bus routes near the Goose are equipped with bike racks to make connecting to trails easier. Get a transit Rider's Guide or call (250) 362–6161. The Web site is www.transitbc.com. **Victoria by Bike and Kayak,** Richard Reeve; phone (250) 744–2801; Web site Victoriabybike.freewebspace.com. **Sooke Cycle & Surf,** 6707 West Coast Road, Sooke, BC V0S 1N0; phone and fax (250) 642–3123; e-mail sookecycle surf@hotmail.com.

Lodging
For additional information you can pick up a brochure called *Sooke Galloping Goose Trail Accommodations* with an area map at a local tourist office. **Goose Trail B&B,** 5341 Sooke Road, Sooke, BC V0S 1N0; toll-free (877) 704–6673; Web site www.GooseTrail BB.com; e-mail stay@goosetrailbb.com. **Snuggery by the Sea,** 5921 Sooke Road, Sooke, BC; phone (250) 642–6423; e-mail dmallett@coastnet.com. **Deertrail Campgrounds Adventure Gateway (Sooke Potholes);** phone (250) 382–3337; Web site www.deer trailresort.com/play; e-mail deertrail@islandnet.com.

Maps/Brochures
Galloping Goose Regional Trail Guide (CRD Parks) by Jim Mulchinock. **Galloping Goose Trail Map** (Greater Victoria Cycling Coalition).

2

Roche Cove Regional Park

This is a pleasant ramble through mixed forest past a creek to a restful but windy cove with a shell beach. The meandering Matheson Creek and Roche Cove are two of the main park highlights. Be aware that the routes leading to viewpoints are as lengthy as the trails themselves. If you don't mind straying off the main trail, which is the Cedar Grove Trail, you can follow the viewpoint signs for a worthwhile look at highlights.

Distance: 4 kilometers (7 km total park trails).
Approximate hiking time: 1½ hours one-way.
Difficulty: Easy.

Elevation gain: 100 meters.
Type of hike: Located about 29 kilometers west from Victoria, this scenic provincial park is situ-

Roche Cove Regional Park

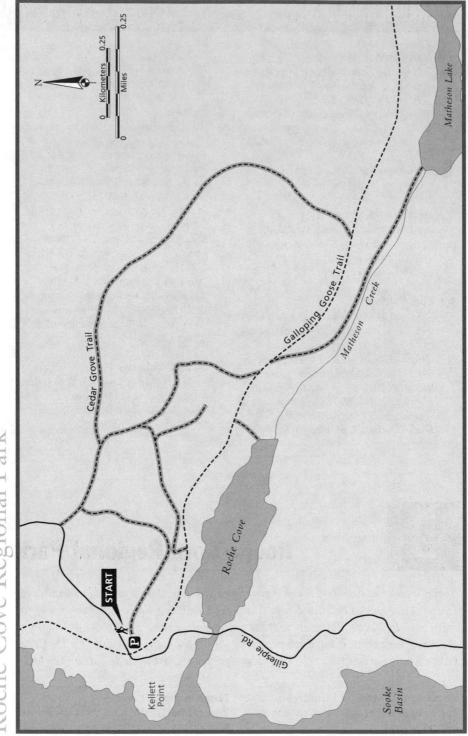

ated in a bustling area of hiking, climbing, and cycling trails, along with popular swimming holes such as Sooke Potholes. Mount Matheson (300 meters) in the nearby Matheson Lake Provincial Park borders Roche Cove, while the 46-kilometer Galloping Goose Regional Trail (Hike 1) that paral-lels Matheson Creek is easily accessed from park trails. Stop by the local info center (2070 Phillips Road) for a detailed trail map.
Best season: Year-round.
Land status: Regional park.

Finding the trailhead: Going west from Victoria on Highway 1 (Trans Canada Highway), take the Colwood, Sooke, Port Renfrew exit (exit 10). Follow Sooke Road (Highway 14) and turn left onto Gillespie Road. The 17 Mile Pub landmark is not far from the corner of Sooke Road and Gillespie Road. The distance from Sooke Road to Roche Cove is 2.8 kilometers. The parking lot for Roche Cove Provincial Park is on the left just after a dip in the road, with Grouse Nest Lodge located to your right. The wide trail that is located to the right of the washrooms at the parking lot is Galloping Goose Regional Trail. There is a small picnic area to the right of this trail. The Cedar Grove Trailhead is located to your left as you enter the parking lot. Look for a small trail heading up through trees. At the trail entrance is a sign on a wood-en post saying TO CEDAR GROVE TRAIL. Four or more offshoots from Cedar Grove Trail are located in the park. These routes aren't marked but indicate at junctions the direction of Cedar Grove Trail.

The hike: Walk uphill into the trees to find the Cedar Grove Trailhead. This part of the trail is dirt with rocky sections and fringed with tall ferns, salal, and alder. About ten minutes into the trail, the road forks at two different places that are right next to each other. Directly to your left is a signpost for Cedar Grove Trail. A sign also indicates a viewpoint straight up a hill. The main trail and sec-ondary routes are short and can be explored at random without losing sight of the main trail. If you decide to turn left at this fork and follow Cedar Grove Trail, parts of this section may be muddy or washed out in spring due to marshy areas. Horseback riders using this trail may overturn portions where skunk cabbage grows in dark, wet soil. In mid-June these areas were still fairly muddy. Logs placed in the middle of the trail will enable you to steer past these sections with little difficulty. Along this route about seven minutes after the first fork, you'll come to another signpost. Take the left fork to follow Cedar Grove Trail uphill.

As you near the creek and cove, you will enter a less rocky, shadier area of the rain forest. To meet Roche Cove, leave the main trail and take a viewpoint route that eventually crosses Galloping Goose Regional Trail. After about eight minutes on this route, you'll notice a mossy bridge crossing over Matheson Creek. This route skirts along the edge of the creek for a bit before heading downhill to a clearing. To your left you'll see a park bench in the midst of broom, grasses, and wildflowers. Cross over Galloping Goose Regional Trail and follow the path that continues on the other side into the forest. Roche Cove is a brief six-minute walk from the Galloping Goose. A signpost indicates

Windswept Roche Cove offers hikers an ideal spot to munch and meditate and a shell beach at low tide.

that the route leads to Matheson Creek. A two-minute walk downhill toward the creek will take you to another signpost. Turn right at the sign that indicates TO MATHESON CREEK AND ROCHE COVE. Take a tributary that fringes the creek. From here, a short scramble down will bring you to the cove. When the tide is low, this shell beach is muddy but still accessible.

To return to the parking lot, take any route going straight up the hill. A three-minute walk uphill to what locals refer to as the Goose should put you at the 34-kilometer mark for this trail. Walk along the Goose going west for about fifteen minutes until you reach the parking lot. Camping is not permitted in the park, and dogs are not allowed on the beach and picnic areas between June 1 and September 15.

Hike Information

Trail Contact
Capital Regional District (CRD) Parks, 490 Atkins Avenue, Victoria, BC V9B 2Z8; phone (250) 478–3344; fax (250) 478–5416; recorded information (250) 474–PARK; Web site www.crd.bc.ca/parks; e-mail crdparks@crd.bc.ca.

Fees/Permits
No fees or permits required.

Local Information
Sooke Visitor Info Center (located beside Sooke Museum), P. O. Box 774, 2070 Phillips Road, Sooke, BC V0S 1N0; phone (250) 642–6351; fax (250) 642–7039.
Sooke-Harbour Chamber of Commerce, 6697 Sooke Road, Sooke, BC V0S 1N0; phone (250) 642–6112; fax (250) 642–7089.

Maps/Brochures
Roche Cove Regional Park brochure.

3

East Sooke Regional Park
Coast Trail

This is a full-day hike over rugged coastline through Douglas fir, western hemlock, and Sitka spruce forest combined with arbutus groves. Reminders of the area's rich past mingle with continuous ocean vistas. Considered one of the Island's most popular wilderness hikes, this rocky seaside climb offers the chance to view a pod of orcas, black-tailed deer, otters, eagles, and turkey vultures that migrate here in fall. Located between Beechey Head and Becher Bay, Alldridge Farm is home to ancient rock carvings that were created by Coast Salish peoples. Recent "petroglyphs" have been added alongside these unique pictures in the way of graffiti.

Distance: 10 kilometers (Coast Trail). East Sooke Regional Park offers more than 50 kilometers of trails with varying levels of difficulty. The Coast Trail is possibly the most traveled (and challenging) due to its spectacular shoreline route.

Approximate hiking time: Between 6 and 8 hours, one-way (Coast Trail).

Difficulty: This hike is rated as challenging due to constant up-and-down motion on rocks.

Type of hike: East Sooke Regional Park is located on 1,422 hectares of land, with Sooke Basin on one side (north) and the Juan de Fuca Strait on the other. This is a rugged hike about an hour from Victoria that winds through fir forest, wildflower meadows, and arbutus groves, and then snakes back to rocky ledges bordering the sea. Pick up a detailed map of the trail systems from the local visitor center located beside the Sooke Regional Museum. The center is about 21 kilometers from East Sooke Regional Park.

Elevation gain: 50 meters.

Best season: May to September. This trail can be hiked throughout the year, but keep in mind that during winter months ice-covered ridges are very slippery. Dense fog may impede a hiker's ability to see the trail at this time of the year, while inland routes may be washed out during a heavy downpour.

Land status: Regional park.

Finding the trailhead: Driving north on Highway 1 (Trans Canada Highway) from Victoria, take the Colwood, Sooke, and Port Renfrew exit (exit 10). Follow Sooke Road (Highway 14) to Gillespie Road, which comes up on your left just after the 17 Mile House Pub landmark located to your right. On Gillespie Road you'll come to the entrance to Roche Cove Regional Park to your left and, shortly after, a bridge that passes by Roche Cove. As you near East Sooke Road, there is a sign to your right that reads EAST SOOKE NATURE'S GALLERY. Stay on Gillespie Road for about 5.8 kilometers until you reach East Sooke Road.

Two main entrances exist in the park for hiking Coast Trail: Pike Road and Aylard Farm. Park information suggests hiking from Pike Road to the entrance at Aylard Farm. Overnight camping is not permitted within the park, and hiking this trail one-way is a full day's journey. Plan to be picked up at the other end, or arrange to take two vehicles, leaving one at the trail's end. Allow thirty minutes of car travel between the two main access points.

East Sooke Regional Park (Coast Trail)

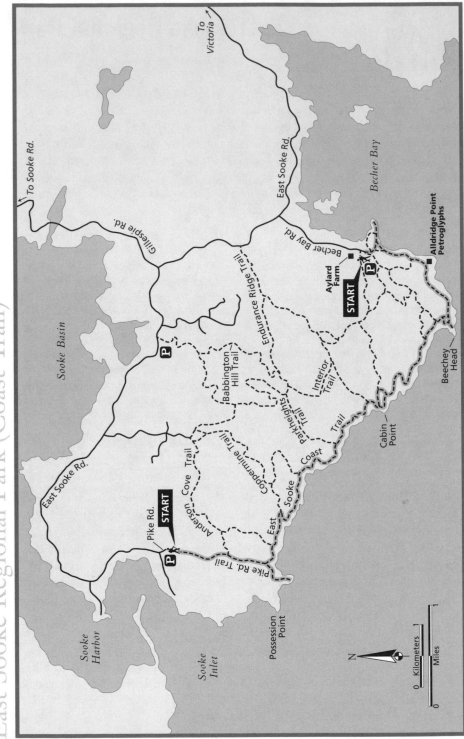

To access the Pike Road entrance, turn right onto East Sooke Road. A sign will indicate Pike Road and Anderson Cove to the right, and Aylard Farm to the left. The Pike Road entrance is about 8.5 kilometers from the junction of Gillespie Road and East Sooke Road. Alternatively, to access the parking lot at Aylard Farm, stay on East Sooke Road, heading south for about 2 kilometers then turning right onto Becher Bay Road to head southwest.

Tidbit Southern Vancouver Island is rich in First Nations history. In this area Coast Salish people fished for salmon and collected roots and berries to sustain them through the winter months.

When you reach the Pike Road entrance, you'll see a large sign that reads, EAST SOOKE REGIONAL PARK PIKE ROAD. There is an upper and a lower parking lot. Leave your vehicle in the lower lot, which is closer to the trailhead. At the far end of the parking lot, opposite the road, is the Pike Road Trailhead. To the right of the trail is an information panel, including a park map. Within the park are group picnicking areas, shelters, toilets, and wheelchair-accessible toilets. Fires are not permitted in the park; dogs and horses are permitted on some of the trails but not in the beach or picnic areas.

The hike: Although rigorous and lengthy, this hike is straightforward in that it mostly follows the coast. Also, tributaries off Coast Trail are well marked with signposts, as is the main trail at all major junctions. Ignore the many offshoots leading inland and stay on the coast. The first section of the trail is a straight, wide path (an old logging road) through lush second-growth forest consisting of green ledges of sword ferns, salmonberry, mosses, and gigantic Douglas fir stumps operating as nurse logs. Follow Pike Road Trail for about half an hour until you reach a gravel cul-de-sac. At this point you will exit the forest and notice glimpses of the ocean through trees. To your right is a public toilet.

At the far end of the circle is a fork. The right fork leads you to a view point of the Juan de Fuca Strait. Follow the signpost indication that shows Coast Trail to the left.

You'll notice that the trail narrows and becomes rocky at this point. There is a sign to your right indicating the area's mining history at Iron Mine Bay. This horseshoe-shaped bay is home to a host of marine life such as sea stars and gooseneck barnacles. Shortly after, you'll pass through cliffside meadows, ferns, mosses, and salmonberry, at which point the trail begins to twist around sharp rocks as it climbs. Pay attention to frequent markers that are posted on rocks along the way. Markers begin after the first Coppermine Trail fork and are usually at critical junctions where the trail takes a turn to the right or left or where the trail ascends into the rocky hillside. If you find that you haven't seen a marker in a while, go back and pick up the trail again from the last one. Notice that markers are only found on rocks along the trail, and not on trees.

Following Iron Mine Bay, you'll come to a left fork that indicates Anderson Cove Trail. The next two forks to the left lead to Coppermine Trail and connect to Interior Trail. Shortly after, Coast Trail meanders inland through a rain forest before meeting the coastline once again. The next fork to the left is Parkheights Trail. After winding to and fro along the coast for a short while, you may detect a little shack on the other side of a valley to the east. The trail travels inland momentarily after this point before bordering the coast again at Cabin Point. A replica of a trap shack was built at Cabin Point to provide visitors with a visual clue as to how fishermen in this area lived and fished many years ago.

When descending from Cabin Point, look to the right of the trail for markers. Many hikers have been known to lose the trail at this point by going straight.

Even on the most beautiful days, nature reminds us of her power, as shown by the raw beauty of this wind-worn tree on Coast Trail in East Sooke Regional Park.

You might notice that some well-meaning hikers have placed sticks over these false routes. Veer right and descend into an open, rocky area. Farther on, the trail descends once again where stonecrop, Indian paintbrush, and nodding onion grow between rocky ledges. Soon the trail ends at a pebble beach and placid cove. Pick up the trail on the east side of this beach, leading into the forest. At this point the trail crosses dense rain forest, waist-high salal, grasses, and ferns.

Continue on the trail going east in the direction of Beechey Head. This spectacular lookout point is worth the short climb to the top—hikers often see whales up here. It is also a well-known spot for observing the fall hawk migration. On a clear day you can see the Olympic Mountains in Olympic National Park to the south. Descend Beechey Head and pick up Coast Trail, once again heading eastward. This portion of the trail closely follows the coast and swings inward on two occasions before arriving at Alldridge Point. Unique petroglyphs characterize this site, which is testimony to the area's strong Coast Salish presence. Continue on to Becher Bay.

At the two extremities of Becher Bay are two distinct left forks that indicate alternate routes to Aylard Farm. You may choose one of these inland shortcuts or continue on to Creyke Point, a scenic bay surrounded by interestingly shaped ridges. At the second left fork (to Aylard Farm) are toilets and a picnic area. If you continue on to Creyke Point, you can take an easterly fork (part of the Coast Trail) to Aylard Farm, which will be on your right as you come back from the point. This is the last fork heading inland to the parking lot. The hike ends at Aylard Farm, a heritage apple orchard and a favorite twilight spot for grazing black-tailed deer.

Options: Although Coast Trail is the longest and most popular of the East Sooke Regional Park trails, here are a few other routes that are worth the effort.

Anderson Cove Trail: Access this trail from Coast Trail. Take the left fork (north) directly after Pike Road Trail winds onto Coast Trail. This trail joins an offshoot trail up to Mount Maguire (272 meters).

Coppermine Trail: This trail passes an old mine site. Access the trail from Coast Trail. From Pike Road Trail take the second fork to the left (north). If you miss it, the third fork also takes you to Coppermine Trail.

Interior Trail: Many routes lead to this trail. This route provides a secondary option if Coast Trail becomes too challenging and/or lengthy. From Pike Road Trail turn left (east) at the first fork. The signpost indicates Anderson Cove Trail. This left fork is about fifteen minutes from the Pike Road Trailhead.

Parkheights Trail: Access this trail from Coast Trail. Turn left (northeast) at the forth fork from the start of Coast Trail.

Endurance Ridge Trail: Access this trail from two main points along Coast Trail. Take the left fork just before arriving at Cabin Point. A second tributary

Mount Finlayson at Goldstream Provincial Park

The trail going up Mount Finlayson is a steep rugged trail with gnarled tree root sections and scrambling on rocks followed by 365-degree ocean and mountain vistas. One of the highest peaks near the capital city of Victoria, Mount Finlayson offers a short but steady climb through second-growth Douglas fir, Garry oak, and arbutus forest. In fall many hikers stop by the Goldstream River to admire the glittering bodies of three species of salmon: chum, coho, and chinook. Up to 50,000 salmon return to spawn in this river each year.

Distance: Close to 2 kilometers to the mountain summit, 4.2 kilometers up and over the other side, and 7.4 kilometers (up and over) with a return trip along Finlayson Arm Road.

Approximate hiking time: This can range from an hour one-way to several hours depending on trail length.

Difficulty: Marked trail sections range from very difficult to moderate due to extremely rugged terrain on certain areas of the mountain. It is inadvisable to enter unmarked areas both for personal safety and to control ecosystem damage.

Type of hike: An easily accessible trailhead in a provincial park 16 kilometers north of downtown Victoria. This trail is great for hikers who lack time but desire an uphill challenge comprised of some climbing on rocks and breathtaking summit views. It's best to wear proper footwear for this trip due to scrambles on rocks. Visitors have the option of hiking up the front of the mountain, up and over the back, or hiking up, over, and returning along the narrow, winding Finlayson Arm Road, which drops steeply from the Highlands down to the Goldstream floodplain.

Elevation gain: 419 meters.

Best season: May to September. Rain, ice, and snow patches appear higher up during winter months.

Land status: Provincial park.

Finding the trailhead: As you drive north on Highway 1 from Victoria, look for signs to Goldstream Provincial Park. On the left you'll pass the campsite area that is open for overnight camping year-round. Stay on Highway 1, then turn right

Signpost

The following is text from a sign found at either side of Mount Finlayson:

"Welcome to Mount Finlayson. The Mount Finlayson Trail threads through extremely sensitive ecosystems. Hikers using trails other than the official, marked trail have a definite and destructive impact on these fragile areas. Mt. Finlayson lies within the Nanaimo Lowlands Ecosection and the Coastal Douglas Fir Biogeoclimatic Zone. Within B.C. less than 3% of this zone is protected. Please stay on the trail marked with orange markers. Damage to these fragile ecosystems will take Nature several decades to repair. Many areas, such as the moss covered rock areas, will take much longer."

Mount Finlayson at
Goldstream Provincial Park

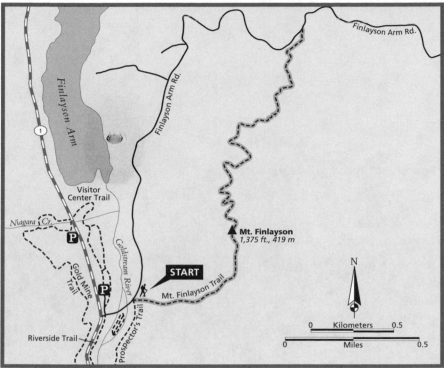

onto Finlayson Arm Road shortly after the campsite turnoff and park in the parking lot near the river. Walk across the bridge to find the trailhead to the right of the road. The trailhead entrance is marked with a covered map and notice panel.

The hike: The trail going up Mount Finlayson starts with a well-worn path threading its way through mostly second-growth Douglas fir forest. It climbs steadily for close to half an hour. The second portion of the trail is scattered with gnarled roots and crushed rock that quickly turns to big rocks. Possibly an old riverbed, this uphill scrambling lasts about half an hour. Orange markings on rocks, along with arrows, clearly show hikers where to climb. The last half hour of the trail includes climbing on rocks through Garry oak and arbutus groves. At this point are a few grassy ledges for resting and snacking before you reach the top. Just before you arrive at the summit, the terrain switches to smooth rock mixed with more climbing between crevices. Pay close attention to orange markers on rock faces. Although it is difficult to lose the trail completely, the trail is not always evident. It once again becomes a dirt path just before the summit and zigzags through arbutus and Garry oak before ambling to the top.

The hike up Mount Finlayson provides views at almost every turn, while sumptuous ocean and mountain views reward the hiker at the summit.

Goldstream Provincial Park has a day-use picnic area and offers campsites that are accessible by vehicle. Contact B.C. Parks for campsite reservations. In spring and summer campers have the use of water taps and hot showers. Self-registration may be in effect during low season. Campfires are allowed during certain times of the year, but there are no electrical hook-ups. Located in the day-use area, Freeman King Visitor Center provides information on the region's natural and cultural history. It has a gift shop and is supported through donations. There is also a viewing deck overlooking the estuary. The estuary itself is part of a no-access quiet zone. This center is open daily in the summer months and from October to February during salmon- and eagle-viewing season.

Key points (km)
0.0   Start at the trailhead off Finlayson Arm Road.

1.8   The trail arrives at a viewpoint on top of Finlayson Peak.

4.2   The trail arrives at Gowland Todd/Finlayson Arm Access Information.

4.3   The trail arrives at Finlayson Arm Road, north of original starting point.

7.4   The trail arrives back at original parking lot via Finlayson Arm Road.

Options: Mount Finlayson is by far the most spectacular hike in Goldstream Provincial Park. There are, however, a few other trails in the park that make up about 16 kilometers. These trails are located on both sides of the Trans Canada Highway (which cuts through the park) and are accessible from several parking lots by vehicle with park facilities close by. The main trails with their times are:

Arbutus Loop: This route goes through an arbutus grove (15 minutes).

Arbutus Ridge: Wildflowers are apparent here in early spring (1½ hours, one-way).

Gold Mine: This trail crosses Niagara Creek to Niagara Falls (47.5-meter falls; 1 hour).

Lower Goldstream: Follow this trail in the fall to view salmon spawning (15 minutes).

Upper Goldstream: This route borders the river and features some of the oldest trees in the park (30 minutes one-way).

Prospector's: Douglas fir, Garry oak, and arbutus forest characterize this trail (1½ hours one-way). Following the Prospector's, Lower Goldstream, Gold-mine, and Arbutus Ridge Trails can make a long circular hike.

Hike Information

🕯 Trail Contact
B.C. Parks: Web site wlapwww.gov.bc. ca/bcparks.

$ Fees/Permits
No fees or permits required.

? Local Information
West Shore Chamber of Commerce, 697 Goldstream Avenue, Victoria, BC V9B 2X2; phone (250) 478–1130; fax (250) 478–1584.

Ⓐ Maps/Brochures
NTS Map 92 B/05.
Goldstream Provincial Park brochure.

Cowichan River Footpath

This easy hike through streamside forests follows the Cowichan River, a popular camping and fishing destination. Located along the trail are Marie Canyon and the 66 Mile Trestle. The 64.4 Mile and Holt Creek Trestles are also spectacular side trips. Spawning salmon may be viewed in season at Skutz Falls. In 1996 the provincial government designated the Cowichan River a B.C. Heritage River to preserve the river's natural environment. While this designation carries no legislative powers, it emphasizes the natural, cultural, and recreational values of the river during land-use planning with an eye toward protecting these values. In keeping with this philosophy, the river was recently nominated as a Canadian Heritage River.

Distance: Up to 20 kilometers of hiking in one direction. Several smaller loops are also possible thanks to angling trails at both ends of the footpath and the new Trans Canada Trail. If you plan to hike the entire footpath, you will need to arrange a pickup for the trailhead at the end of your hike.
Approximate hiking time: 6 to 7 hours.
Difficulty: Easy with limited steep sections.
Type of hike: A forested footpath laced with roots and bedrock. The trail is well marked with signs indicating park boundaries and distances from the Glenora Trailhead.
Elevation gain: The footpath has limited steep sections near the Skutz Falls Trailhead and where the path joins the Trans Canada Trail.
Best season: Year-round. Hikers visiting during September and October will be rewarded with fall colors thanks to an abundance of big-leaf maples.
Land status: Provincial park and First Nations lands.

Finding the trailhead: Cowichan River Footpath has three access points. The southeast access is located in Glenora, 3 kilometers outside Duncan. Traveling south on Highway 1 through Duncan, turn right (west) onto Miller Road. Turn left onto Glenora Road and continue through the village of Glenora. Once past the Glenora Community Hall, watch for Vaux Road on your right. Follow Vaux Road (it becomes Robertson Road) to its end and park at the Cowichan Fish and Game Association Shooting Range. The trailhead is located several hundred meters beyond the parking lot. This access point will also link you up with the Cowichan River portion of the Trans Canada Trail.

Big-Leaf Maple

The big-leaf maple *(Acer macrophyllum)* is the largest and fastest-growing maple in Canada. First Nations people traditionally used the tree's wood for dishes, pipes, clothing hooks, and paddles, and the inner bark for ropes and baskets. They also ate the young shoots and made a type of boiled syrup from the sap.

Cowichan River Footpath

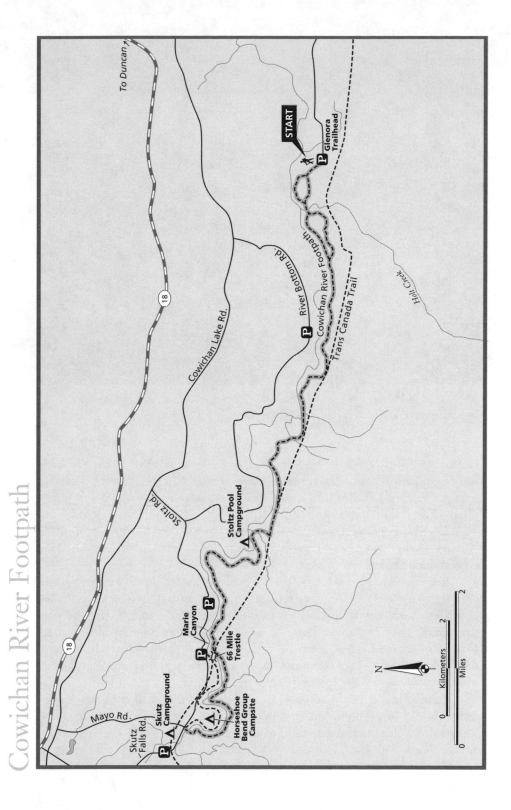

This boardwalk section of the Cowichan River Footpath allows hikers to enjoy the lush rainforest without encroaching on the fragile environment.

The middle access is located near the 66 Mile Trestle. Heading north on Highway 1 from Duncan, turn left (west) onto the Cowichan Valley Highway and continue for approximately 15 kilometers until you reach the Highway 18 connector. Turn left. At Old Cowichan Lake Road, turn left again and follow the road until it intersects with Stoltz Road. Turn right onto Stoltz Road, right onto Riverbottom Road, and follow the signs to the 66 Mile Trestle. You can also access the Skutz Falls Trailhead by continuing along Riverbottom Road and crossing the bridge via Skutz Falls Forest Service Road.

The western access is located at the Skutz Falls Trailhead. Heading north on Highway 1 from Duncan, turn left (west) onto the Cowichan Valley Highway. Turn left at Skutz Falls Road where signs indicate the route to Cowichan River Provincial Park. Continue along the route until you meet Mayo Road and a bridge across the river. Parking is available on both sides of the bridge, though space is limited on the south side. A map and a provincial park display indicate the location of the trailhead.

Camping facilities are available on a seasonal basis at Skutz Falls, beginning May 15 and ending on September 5, and year-round at Stoltz Pool. Reservations are accepted at the Stoltz Pool campsite only. Water is available at both campsites. All other water consumed along the trail must be boiled, filtered, or treated.

At both ends of Cowichan River Footpath, you will see signs marking the Trans Canada Trail (TCT). This segment of the 16,000-kilometer TCT parallels Cowichan River Footpath via the old railway that was used to connect Victoria with the timberlands of the Cowichan Valley. Though shorter and straighter than Cowichan River Footpath, this portion of the TCT is less scenic and is better suited to horseback riders and cyclists traveling the corridor to and from Lake Cowichan.

Tidbit The distance markers on this portion of the Trans Canada Trail refer back to the days of the Canadian Northern Pacific Railway—now the Canadian National Railway—and measure the number of miles to Victoria.

The hike: Now used extensively by hikers, Cowichan River Footpath was constructed in the 1960s by the Cowichan Fish and Game Association to help anglers access portions of the 35-kilometer-long Cowichan River.

After the first kilometer, the trail crosses Holt Creek Bridge just upstream from where the creek enters the Cowichan River. Farther upstream on the Trans Canada Trail, a trestle spans 73 meters over the creek. This is the first of three scenic trestles on the TCT worth the extra mileage for a side trip or a photo opportunity. Beyond the bridge the main footpath meets up with the first of many angling trails offering a closer look at the river. Following either fork will take you in the right direction, though the right option is the more scenic of the two. Watch for large examples of western red cedar and western yew as you make your way along the trail.

At approximately 3.5 kilometers, the trail passes through Picnic Grounds Pool. Mossy terrain and grassy streamside banks offer several places for a rest stop or a quick snack. Throughout early spring and summer, skunk cabbage also adds color to the many meandering brooks. Its characteristic pungent odor is certain to reach you.

Just before the midpoint of the trail, houses begin to appear on the opposite bank. The trail rises sharply, joining the TCT and circumventing private property. While this segment is flat and relatively unimpressive, it offers a glimpse of the old Canadian Northern Pacific Railway established in 1911. After less than a kilometer, the footpath leaves the TCT and heads back down to the river's edge, passing through maple and alder forest.

Beyond the junction, the trail intersects an open area where dirt bikes have partially obliterated the footpath. This is Stoltz Flats and is located directly across from the Stoltz Pool Campground. Continue straight along the river's edge, taking care to avoid sections where erosion has sloughed the bank. Farther upstream, steep cliffs offer an impressive cross section of riverside geology. This experience is replayed again at approximately 14.5 kilometers when the trail turns uphill and heads away from the river along a series of steep

Sahtlam Lodge

The Sahtlam Lodge, located at kilometer 9.9 on the opposite side of the river, offers maps, information, and occasionally transports guests to portions of the trail including sections of Marie Canyon and 10 kilometers of riverside walking. Guests are also invited to use the lodge's private river cart to access the trail independently. For more information on Sahtlam Lodge and Cabins, contact (250) 748–7738 or e-mail cabins@sahtlamlodge.com.

switchbacks. The top of the bluff affords a good view of the striped sedimentary rock comprising much of the gorge. This also marks the beginning of the 2-kilometer-long Marie Canyon.

While the footpath doesn't cross the 66 Mile Trestle, the trail does intersect the TCT at this scenic viewpoint, offering footpath hikers the opportunity to walk the 90-meter-long bridge and view the gorge from a height of 35 meters. The trestle is a recent addition to the TCT and provides an alternate route to the Skutz Falls Trailhead. If you are interested in hiking the opposite side of the river, cross the trestle and pick up North Side Trail to Skutz Falls. The picnic grounds on the opposite side of the gorge also provide an opportunity to rest and take in the scenery. A portion of North Side Trail crosses land belonging to Cowichan Tribes.

For those continuing along the footpath, watch for gnarled Garry oaks hugging the cliff's edge. Garry oaks and the flowers that grow beneath them once thrived on the dry rocky slopes of southern Vancouver Island. While development and resource extraction pushed these ecosystems to the brink of extinction, many Garry oak meadows are now receiving much-needed protection. The stand located across from the Horseshoe Bend Campsite is the most westerly stand of Garry oaks on Vancouver Island. Stick to the path as you pass and refrain from picking wildflowers.

Following the meadow is a series of steep switchbacks. This signals the final leg of your hike and provides more views of the canyon. The hike officially ends at the Skutz Falls parking lot, though further angling trails extend up river across Skutz Falls Forest Service Road. Attractions at Skutz Falls include eight fish ladders and a day-use area.

Key points (km)

0.0 Start at the Glenora Trailhead located beyond the parking lot of the Cowichan Fish and Game Association.

0.8 The trail changes from a gravel path into a forest trail.

1.0 The trail arrives at the Glenora Trailhead and Skutz Falls Trailhead junction. Continue down the hill.

1.3 The trail crosses the Holt Creek Bridge. Immediately after crossing, the trail forks, offering an alternative along Angler's Loop. Turn right to stay closer to the water.

2.9   Angler's Loop rejoins the upper footpath.

3.7   The trail reaches the Picnic Grounds Pool.

3.9   The trail reaches the Eagle's Roost Picnic Ground.

7.7   The trail passes an active beaver dam on your right.

8.8   The trail crosses the Fuller Falls Bridge.

8.9   The trail passes through Bear Hollow.

9.8   Cowichan River Footpath merges with the Trans Canada Trail and follows a flat railway grade.

9.9   A spur leaves the main trail on your right. This side trail leads to the Sahtlam Lodge and Cabins.

10.7   The footpath leaves the Trans Canada Trail and returns to the forest.

11.0   The trail reaches Summit Creek.

14.4   The trail reaches Mosquito Run. Watch for characteristic sedimentary rock.

14.8   The trail reaches the Marie Canyon Waterfall.

15.0   The trail reaches the 66 Mile Trestle over Marie Canyon. For a scenic lookout and the option of hiking on the other side of the river, turn right.

17.5   The trail passes through a grove of Garry oaks.

20.0   The trail ends at the Skutz Falls Trailhead.

Hike Information

Trail Contacts
B.C. Parks: Web site wlapwww.gov.bc.ca/bcparks.
The Trails Society of British Columbia, 425–1367 West Broadway, Vancouver, BC V6H 4A9; phone (604) 737–3188; fax (604) 738–7175; Web site www.trails bc.ca/faq.html; e-mail trailsbc@trailsbc.ca.

Fees/Permits
B.C. Parks charges a fee of $12 per party to stay in the campgrounds located on Cowichan River Footpath. While Skutz Falls is open seasonally from May 15 to September 4, the Stolz Pool camping area is open year-round.

Local Information
Duncan Cowichan Visitor Info Center, 381A Trans Canada Highway, Duncan, BC V9L 3R5; phone (250) 746–4636 or (250) 748–1111; fax (250) 746–8222; Web site www.duncancc.bc.ca; e-mail visitorinfo@duncancc.bc.ca.
Sahtlam Lodge and Cabins, 5720 Riverbottom Road West, Duncan, BC V9L 6H9; phone (250) 748–7738; Web site www.SahtlamLodge.com; e-mail cabins@sahtlamlodge.com.

Mount Tzouhalem

Overlooking Maple Bay in the Cowichan Valley, also known as "the warm land," Mount Tzouhalem offers trails with viewpoints and wildflower meadows. The Mount Tzouhalem Ecological Reserve offers seasonal opportunities to view Garry oak meadows and their associated wildflowers, including blue camas, spring gold, shooting star, and wild sunflowers. The hike up to the white cross provides views of the Cowichan Valley.

Distance: Variations up to 10 kilometers.

Difficulty: Easy to moderate. The area is criss-crossed with roads and mountain biking trails.

Type of hike: Mount Tzouhalem offers several hiking and walking opportunities, ranging from easy strolls along grassy footpaths to steeper climbs via disused roads and trails.

Elevation gain: Varies depending on the trail. Mount Tzouhalem is 480 meters high.

Best season: The Mount Tzouhalem Ecological Reserve is best viewed at the height of the Garry oak wildflower season in April and May. While hiking in the reserve is discouraged, a careful walk to view this breathtaking example of a Garry oak meadow is allowed in the company of a guide. To arrange a guided visit, contact the Cowichan Valley Naturalists Society at (250) 746–6659.

Land status: Ecological reserve and private lands.

Finding the trailhead: From Duncan, follow Highway 1 to Trunk Road. Turn left (east) and head through Cowichan Tribes territory (Trunk Road will become Tzouhalem Road) until the junction with Maple Bay Road. Turn left onto Maple Bay Road and drive 3 kilometers to Kingsview Road. This is the entrance to "The Properties," a hilltop development on the west side of Mount Tzouhalem. Turn right onto Kingsview Road and follow the road through Chippewa, and finally Kaspa. Park at the end of Kaspa Road.

The hike: While many of the hikes on Mount Tzouhalem follow roads and unmaintained footpaths, we decided to include this location as a representative sample of Garry oak meadows on Vancouver Island. Outside the reserve, a walk to the southwest viewpoint also offers views and a slice of local history. The dis-

Ecological Reserves

Ecological reserves offer opportunities for scientists and schools to study rare and endangered plants and animals. While they are not parks, they are protected under the B.C. Ecological Reserves Program and administered by B.C. Parks.

Mount Tzouhalem

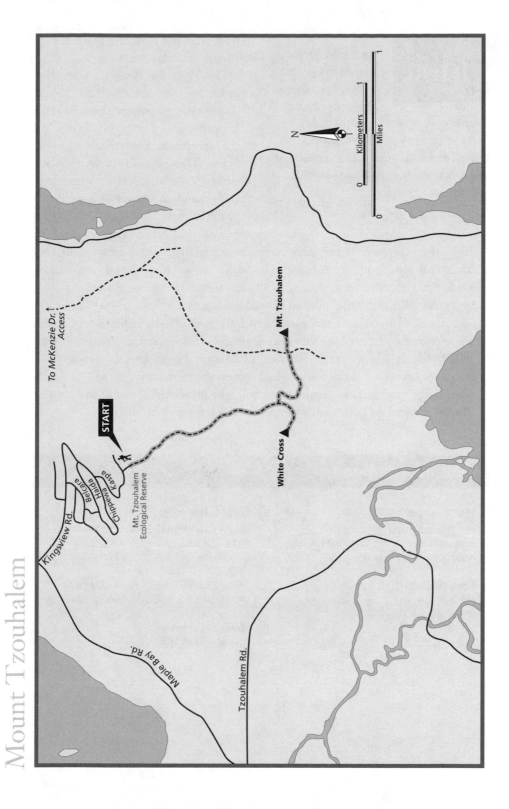

trict does not maintain the trails on Mount Tzouhalem.

In 1976 the Sisters of St. Ann erected a wooden cross on Mount Tzouhalem to inspire them in their annual Good Friday pilgrimage up the mountain from their convent below. The cross was replaced in the early 1990s with today's white iron replica and continues to inspire pilgrims to make the yearly climb from St. Ann's Church parking lot. To reach the viewpoint at the white cross, walk uphill to the junction and take Municipal Road on your right. This road passes the Mount Tzouhalem Ecological Reserve. Please obey signs and stay off the reserve unless accompanied by a guide. When the trail meets a disused road, turn left. Take the next right and hike uphill until you see a trail marked with flagging. This trail heads west to the white cross. Be prepared for the many trails and offshoots crisscrossing the area.

The development at the bottom of Mount Tzouhalem known as The Properties owns an additional 120 hectares on the mountain that will be developed in the future. This development will take place to the east of the current subdivision and will eventually tie in with the Lakeview Subdivision.

Hike Information

📞 Trail Contact
For information on the Ecological Preserve, contact the **Cowichan Valley Naturalists Society** at (250) 746–6659.

💲 Fees/Permits
No fees or permits required.

❓ Local Information
Duncan Cowichan Visitor Info Center, 381A Trans Canada Highway, Duncan, BC V9L 3R5; phone (250) 746–4636 or (250) 748–1111; fax (250) 746–8222; Web site www.duncancc.bc.ca; e-mail visitorinfo@duncancc.bc.ca.

 Maps/Brochures
NTS Map 92B/13.

8

Maple Mountain

Five connecting trails provide a variety of opportunities to explore Maple Mountain's rocky bluffs, dense forests, and stunning viewpoints. The Blue, Pink, Yellow, and Orange Trails offer spectacular views of Salt Spring, Thetis, and Kuper Islands, along with Sansum Narrows. Watch for clusters of Garry oaks and rocky bluffs spotted with moss and wildflowers (in season). The Maple Mountain trails are located in a municipal forest reserve managed by the District of North Cowichan. The forest reserve is a working community forest that provides revenues for the municipality from its land base, as well as recreation and forestry education opportunities. These lands have been in the municipal forest reserve since 1946.

Distances and approximate hiking times (one-way):

- *Blue Trail:* 5 kilometers—2½ hours.
- *Green Trail:* 2.5 kilometers—30 minutes.
- *Pink Trail:* 3.7 kilometers—2 hours.
- *Orange Trail:* 3.2 kilometers—2 hours.
- *Yellow Trail:* 4 kilometers—2 hours.

Difficulty: Moderate. While the Green Trail is an easy walk through second-growth forest, the Blue Trail includes slippery log crossings and steep cliffs overlooking Sansum Narrows. Both the Orange and Pink Trails include steep climbs up to the main viewing area.

Type of hike: A forested footpath passing over slippery logs with sections of steep and narrow climbing. Some trails contain portions of old roads degenerating into cobble walkways.

Elevation gain: Varies depending on the trail. The Pink Trail is the steepest of the five hikes on Maple Mountain, rising to a height of 500 meters.

Best season: Year-round. Hikers visiting Maple Mountain in April or May will be rewarded with colorful displays of wildflowers, including blue camas, spring gold, and blue-eyed Mary.

Land status: Municipal forest reserve.

Finding the trailhead: Traveling south on Highway 1 from Nanaimo, access the Chilco Road Trailhead by turning left at the Salt Spring Ferry turnoff and then left again onto Chemainus Road. Follow the route through the community of the Halalt First Nation and turn right onto Crofton Road. After Crofton Road becomes Chaplin Street, turn right onto York Avenue (which becomes Osborne Bay Road), and then turn left onto Chilco Road. Drive to the end of Chilco Road, keeping to the right fork, and park off to the side, just before the gate, taking care not to block the road for emergency access. For those traveling north from Duncan, access the trail via Herd Road, which intersects Osborne Bay Road just before Maple Bay.

For the Arbutus Avenue/Maple Mountain Road access, follow Highway 1 to Herd Road. Turn east and follow Herd Road until it intersects Maple Bay Road. Turn left onto Maple Bay Road and head down the hill to the ocean. At the foot of the hill, turn left onto Beaumont Road and follow the winding route for approximately a kilometer (it becomes Arbutus Avenue). Watch for a sign on your left indicating the Orange Trail. Farther along Arbutus Avenue, turn

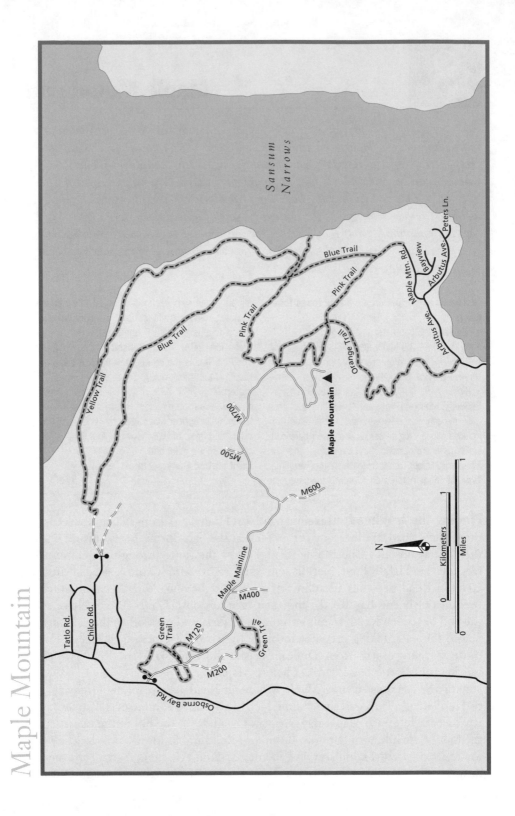

Maple Mountain

left onto Maple Mountain Road and continue along until the end. There is a small parking area and markers indicating the Blue Trail.

To access trails via Osborne Bay Road, follow Highway 1 to Herd Road and turn east. Turn left where Herd Road intersects Osborne Bay Road and drive until you see the signs indicating the Maple Mountain Forest Reserve. The Green Trail begins approximately 400 meters past the gate, which is usually locked on weekends, during the summer months, and during periods of high fire hazard. Park at the gate and walk the road to the trailhead. If the gate is open, you may also drive to the main viewing point near the peak of Maple Mountain and access the Pink and Orange Trails from a higher elevation.

The hike(s): In addition to being a popular hiking area, Maple Mountain is crisscrossed with mountain biking trails. At the time of publication, color-coded flagging tape and sporadic signage marked the five official hiking trails in this municipal forest reserve and community forest.

The Blue Trail: The Blue Trail is the longest of the Maple Mountain trails and offers views of Saltspring Island and Sansum Narrows. Starting at the Chilco Road access, locate the Blue Trail beyond the water tower, approximately 300 meters from the gate. A fork with misleading signage indicates the start of the trail. Turn left at this fork and head down a wide path into forests dominated by western red cedar and Douglas fir. Follow trail markers and flagging tape through a wonderland of mature forest, log bridges, and mountain biking offshoots. The trail winds around the east side of the mountain, intersecting with the Pink Trail (twice), crossing under the power lines, and ending at Maple Mountain Road.

The Pink Trail: Climbing a distance of nearly 500 meters to the peak of Maple Mountain, the Pink Trail is the steepest of the Maple Mountain hikes, providing some of the choicest views. Find the Pink Trail at one of two places where it intersects the southern portion of the Blue Trail beyond the Maple Mountain Road access. The trail will take you through rocky terrain and sparse forests and down to the edge of Sansum Narrows.

The Orange Trail: Locate the Orange Trail via the Arbutus Avenue access or (if the gate is open) via Maple Mountain Main at the upper parking lot. The Orange Trail winds from a residential area, beneath power lines, to the main viewing area looking out over Saltspring Island and Sansum Narrows. Various

The Manzanita

Watch for a middle-growing shrub called the hairy manzanita as the trails skirt open rocky meadows. The manzanita or *Arctostaphylos columbiana* is a native shrub characteristic of dry-climate bluffs like those found on Maple Mountain. In early spring the tips of these middle-growing plants burst into fragrant buds much loved by bees.

As the Blue Trail winds around Maple Mountain, be on the lookout for glorious views of Salt Spring Island and Sansum Narrows.

viewpoints exist along this route, which progresses from a steep path to an old road, including some down to Somenos and Quamichan Lake in the southwest, and others down to Maple Bay in the south. If starting at the Arbutus Avenue access, take note that parking is extremely limited.

The Green Trail: The easiest and shortest of the routes, the Green Trail begins at the foot of Maple Mountain and cuts a small arc through the forest. If the gate is open where Maple Mountain Main intersects Osborne Bay Road, drive half a kilometer up the road and park where signs denote the start of the Green Trail.

The Yellow Trail: The Yellow Trail begins and ends on the Blue Trail, paralleling the Blue Trail's route at a lower elevation.

Hike Information

Trail Contact
District of North Cowichan, Box 278, 7030 Trans Canada Highway, Duncan, BC V9L 3X4; phone (250) 746–3100; fax (250) 746–3133; Web site www.northcowichan.bc.ca.

Fees/Permits
No fees or permits required.

Local Information
Duncan Cowichan Visitor Info Center, 381A Trans Canada Highway, Duncan, BC V9L 3R5; phone (250) 746–4636 or (250) 748–1111; fax (250) 746–8222; Web site www.duncancc. bc.ca; e-mail visitorinfo@duncancc.bc.ca.

Maps/Brochures
NTS Map 92B/13.

Cable Bay Nature Trail and Dodd Narrows

A bark mulch path ambles through immature temperate rain forest with some old-growth Douglas fir trees and ocean views. The forest is clear-cut on both sides of this protected area. Although the official trail ends at the bridge, the hike continues past this point to Dodd Narrows. This is a great place for spotting sea lions, pods of orcas, and eagles.

Distance: 3.7 kilometers.
Approximate hiking time: 1½ hours one-way.
Difficulty: Easy.
Type of hike: Accessible 440-hectare park with wooden steps, gravel, and stone paths.

Elevation gain: No significant elevation gain.
Best season: June to September. The trail may be muddy in winter months.
Land status: Regional park.

Finding the trailhead: From Nanaimo, take Highway 1 (Trans Canada Highway) south to the first Cedar Road exit. Drive along Cedar Road until you come to MacMillan Road. Follow MacMillan Road for about half a kilometer and turn right (east) onto Holden-Corso Road. Holden-Corso Road ascends a hill and veers right, becoming Barnes Road. Continue east on Barnes Road to Nichola Road. Watch for signage to the Cable Bay Nature Trail along the road. Follow Nichola Road north approximately another half a kilometer to the parking lot at Cable Bay.

The hike: Once at the trailhead, follow the path beneath power lines and into the forest. From time to time you'll see other trails and logging roads winding through the woods and crisscrossing the trail. Stay on the main trail, which is broad and well marked with park signs on wooden posts. About half an hour from the parking lot, you'll arrive at Cable Bay. Continue on past the small bridge where the Cable Bay Trail officially ends. The second section of this walk follows a narrow seaside path along the Northumberland Channel to Dodd Narrows. From the footbridge to Dodd Narrows is 1.7 kilometers. You will notice that the seascape becomes more spectacular, with a greater diversity of plant life.

> **Tidbit**
>
> Dodd Narrows is considered one of the hottest dive sites in British Columbia. The strong currents of 8 to 9 knots in this channel attract a large assortment of marine species such as sea anemone, aggregating anemone, king crab, sea stars, orange cup corals, and rockfish and cod. California and Steller's sea lions can also be found feasting in this channel.

Cable Bay Nature Trail and Dodd Narrows

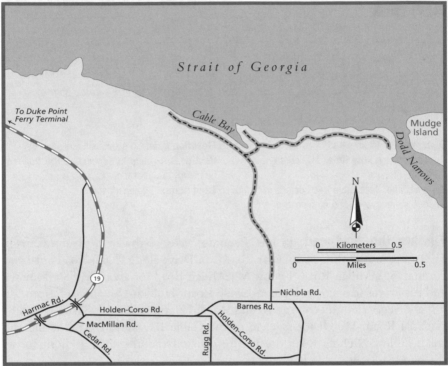

Take the right fork after the small bridge at Cable Bay. The trail will meander with fairly consistent ocean views. From this vantage point, you will notice Nanaimo and Duke Point (one of the Island's newest ferry terminals). Remain on the well-trod trail until you come to a white beacon with a ladder attached. From here you can see a few of the Gulf Islands to the south, including Mudge Island and Gabriola Island.

Hike Information

 Trail Contact
Nanaimo Parks, Recreation and Culture, 500 Bowen Road, Nanaimo, BC V9R 1Z7; phone (250) 756–5200.

 Local Information
Tourism Nanaimo, Beban House, 2290 Bowen Road, Nanaimo, BC V9T 3K7; phone (250) 756–0106.

 Fees/Permits
No fees or permits required.

Lush western red cedar forest shelters the hiker on the Cable Bay Nature Trail.

10

Piper's Lagoon Park

Built on an isthmus that stretches out to a rocky headland, this eight-hectare park fea-tures snaking trails through mixed forest to a number of seaside lookouts. Piper's Lagoon Park is one of the ideal spots in the area to enjoy fiery orange and purple sunsets. Artists often congregate here to paint the landscape. Another favorite activity is bird-watching; seagulls, sandpipers, horned grebes, loons, kingfishers, bald eagles, and great blue herons are just a few of the varieties of bird life found here. If hiker's luck is on your side, you might see a migrating pod of orcas or sea lions basking on the rocks.

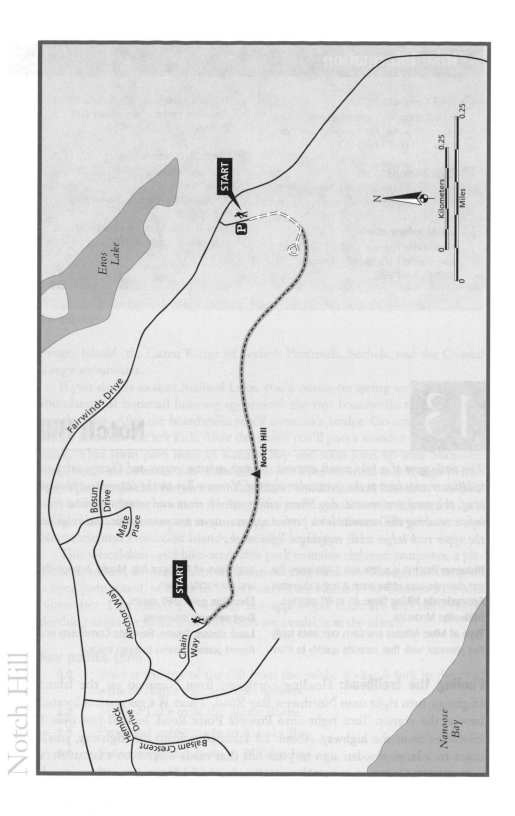

Notch Hill parking lot. There's a large sign indicating the trailhead, though the entrance is slightly concealed from the road. Park your car in the parking lot and look for a map board that is located to the right of the trailhead.

The hike: Ascending to a lookout over Nanoose Bay, Notch Hill offers a morning or afternoon hike through immature and Garry oak forests. Frequent secondary trails bypass this area. To minimize damage to fragile wildflowers, keep to the main trail.

From the parking lot, follow a wide gravel road past a metal gate. You'll go by a facility building and a narrow trail heading into the woods on your left. Pass this trail and follow a path along the left side of two circular holding tanks. You'll soon meet another trail coming down the hill that intersects the trail you're on. Stay on the main trail that veers right into Garry oak and arbutus forest and you'll come to a second trail fork. Take the left fork, which ambles along the bank, instead of the one that ascends. A little farther along the bank, you'll witness a spectacular example of an older arbutus tree. This is also the location of the first viewpoint of Nanoose Bay and the surrounding area.

Continuing upward, the trail veers right and enters denser and shadier mixed forest. Waist-high sword ferns fan the trail at a few spots, and a small footbridge crosses a potentially muddy area. As you continue to ascend, you'll notice that the well-trod path is strewn with arbutus leaves and that mosses border the trail. When you enter the clearing, note the wire fence marking the boundary of this property. This location offers a picturesque place to rest and enjoy the view. Alternatively, follow the trail down to the other side of the hill where the hike ends at Chain Way.

Key points (km)

0.0	Start at the Notch Hill Trailhead and parking lot.
0.3	The trail skirts to the left past two large circular holding tanks.
0.4	The trail comes to second fork. Take the left fork. In the distance you'll see a spectacular example of an older arbutus tree.
0.87	The trail meets up with a small footbridge.
1.0	The trail reaches Notch Hill.

Options: Pick up a trail map at the Fairwinds Center, located on Fairwinds Drive just past the Notch Hill Trailhead. A number of other short trails exist in the vicinity, meandering through the Fairwinds property and subdivisions. While Notch Hill provides some of the best views and glimpses of wildflowers, some of these trails offer a closer look at local lakes and lower-elevation forests. The hikes following subdivision roads are not listed here: Enos Lake Loop: 1.2 kilometers; Meadow Loop: 1 kilometer; Enos Connector: 1.6 kilometers; Enos

Creek Loop: 2.2 kilometers; Swallow Trail: 0.8 kilometer; Enchanted Forest: 1.8 kilometers; Fairwinds Connector: 1.5 kilometers; David's Lookout: 1.1 kilometers.

Hike Information

🕐 Trail Contact
Fairwinds Community and Resort, 3455 Fairwinds Drive, Nanoose Bay, BC V9P 9K6; phone (250) 468–5303; fax (250) 468–9840.

❓ Fees/Permits
No fees or permits required.

❓ Local Information
Tourism Nanaimo, Beban House, 2290 Bowen Road, Nanaimo, BC V9T 3K7; phone (250) 756–0106.

🔼 Maps/Brochures
NTS Map 92F/08.
Fairwinds Community and Resort Private Recreational Trails map.

South Island Honorable Mentions

Sooke Potholes Provincial Park

This trail follows a gravel road from a privately owned campsite bordering the Sooke River. Most of the large pools or potholes formed from rock edging the river are found at the end of the trail. Hike this trail if you wish to visit these geologically unique potholes, or if you happen to be cycling the nearby Galloping Goose Regional Trail (Hike 1). The Goose runs through this park on its last leg to Leechtown just past Rippling Rock Beach and a gravel pit to your left. You'll see caution signs for park vehicles and a sign on the trail itself designating it as multiuse. A parking lot is located just past this point for users of the Goose. Vehicles use this trail as a year-round access route to the campground. The trail is 5 kilometers one-way with an elevation gain of about 350 meters. It takes about an hour to an hour and a half to reach the end. To locate the trailhead, travel north from Victoria on Highway 1 (Trans Canada Highway) and take the Colwood, Sooke, and Port Renfrew exit (exit 10). Follow Sooke Road (Highway 14). Turn right onto Sooke River Road. If you cross a bridge and pass the Castle Pub with the red roof on your left, you've gone too far. The distance from the Sooke Road and Sooke River Road junction to the Sooke Potholes Provincial Park parking lot is about 5 kilometers.

◄ *The arbutus tree grows on the Island's south coast, often on rocky outcrops overlooking the ocean. An evergreen, the tree sheds its reddish-brown bark instead of its leaves and produces clusters of white flowers in the spring.*

The parking lot is very busy in summer due to the area's reputation as a local swimming hole. Be advised that vehicles not in designated parking areas will be towed. The trail starts to the right of a green entrance booth located in the parking lot. For more information, contact B.C. Parks, wlapwww.gov.bc.ca/bcparks. For details about campground fees and schedules, contact Deertrail Campgrounds, Suite 190–3795 Carey Road, Victoria, BC V8Z 6T8; phone (250) 382–DEER (3337); Web site www.deertrail@islandnet.com.

Kludahk Trail/San Juan Ridge

The Kludahk Trail runs parallel to the Juan de Fuca Marine Trail at a higher elevation along the San Juan Ridge for approximately 50 kilometers. The trail can be accessed via a number of logging roads from Sooke, Jordan River, and Port Renfrew, and is best hiked starting in late June. Though characteristically known as a trail, much of this hike is actually a route that requires map and compass skills and a solid sense of direction. There is little or no flagging on the route, and some sections can be extremely wet. There is also a 10-meter-high ladder between Walker and Wye Lakes. Active logging may cut down on access during the summer. Once on the ridge, hikers typically see delicate subalpine meadows, hemlock forests, and mountain lakes. The Kludahk Club maintains a number of cabins on this route, and you must obtain permission before using them. For more information contact the Kludahk Outdoors Club, 2037 Kaltasin Road, Sooke, BC V0S 1N0; phone (250) 642–3523.

Ammonite Falls

Visit this area in the rainy seasons of late fall, winter, or spring to see the spectacular 24-meter falls. Part of the Benson Creek Falls Regional Park system, this pleasant but challenging 2.7-kilometer hike (one-way) through mostly Douglas fir forest (with surrounding clear-cuts) and over creek crossings offers an optional steep drop to Benson Creek. The trail elevation is 120 meters, while the hiking time is about an hour one-way. To find the trailhead, travel north from Nanaimo on the Nanaimo Parkway (Highway 19) until you come to Jingle Pot Road (exit 18). Heading west, turn left onto Kilpatrick Road and right onto Jameson Road. Watch for a yellow gate at the end of Jameson Road (before the intersection with Northwood Road), which marks the trailhead. The wide gravel road will cross a creek at the beginning. Shortly after, it climbs uphill, passes a logging road on the left, and narrows. A trail comes up on your right that is marked with flagging. Follow this meandering trail up a bank and down a steep descent until you come to a firepit. To access the falls, go down a steep path to the left of the firepit. There are ropes to assist you down the ravine. The point at which people may get lost on this hike is at 1 kilometer from the trailhead, where the forest access road swings to the left. At this point you must leave the main road and keep straight ahead. For more information, contact Tourism Nanaimo, Beban House, 2290 Bowen Road, Nanaimo, BC V9T 3K7; phone (250) 756–0106.

Mid-
Island

The mid-island area encompasses the cities of Parksville-Qualicum to the south and Courtenay/Comox and Campbell River to the north. Within this region lies Strathcona Park, the largest park on Vancouver Island, as well as a plethora of boot-tested hiking opportunities along the ocean, fresh water, and up mountain peaks.

One of the largest parks in the province (250,000 hectares), Strathcona Park is a veritable gold mine for hikers seeking a backcountry experience. Home to the highest peak on Vancouver Island, the highest waterfall in North America, and some of the finest examples of alpine wildflowers seen in the province, Strathcona Park is a gem of extremes, offering everything from short jaunts to rigorous, multiday expeditions. Primary access to the park is via the central island cities of Campbell River, Courtenay/Comox, and Port Alberni.

Wherever you choose to hike in Strathcona Park, remember that snow may linger at higher elevations well into summer, and weather may shift quickly and without warning, bringing on precipitation and sharp changes in temperature. Always carry warm clothing and emergency supplies. Topographic maps and the skills to use them are an absolute must when hiking ridge routes.

Taking along proper rain gear, a water filter, sunglasses, and a camera will also go a long way toward enhancing and preserving your Strathcona experience. Backcountry camping is permitted 1 kilometer beyond main roads or, where available, at designated sites. The park also offers group and single-site campsites and camping areas accessible only by water. Overnight fees apply at most camping areas. Park officials recommend that anyone wishing to explore unmarked areas or stay overnight leave an itinerary with a family member, a friend, or a park official. Dogs and other pets are not permitted in backcountry areas for a variety of good reasons, which include the life and death of you, your pet, and backcountry wildlife. Fires are permitted only in designated areas. Be sure to check with the park staff or one of the contacts listed beneath the hike descriptions for recent trail conditions. These conditions are also available on-line at wlapwww.gov.bc.ca/bcparks/explore/parkpgs/strathcn/trail_updates.pdf. The information available from these sources is essential for making your trip into Strathcona safe, positive, and memorable.

14 Englishman River/Morrison Creek

For an afternoon or half-day nature walk, a hike along the picturesque Englishman River and its tributaries offers a diversity of ecological systems. Start with a steep descent and a slippery log crossing at the end of Englishman River Road and continue on to level trails and a tour of the Englishman River Salmon Enhancement Project. Follow this trail in spring and you may just see carpets of fawn lilies, coltsfoot, and bleeding heart nestled in among mature alder trees. Thanks to local beavers, this hike provides year-round bird-watching opportunities in the surrounding wetlands. Great horned owls, great blue herons, and myriad songbirds are just some of the area's inhabitants.

Distance: More than 6 kilometers of trail.
Approximate hiking time: 2- to 3-hour loop.
Difficulty: Easy. The lower portion of the trail involves a log crossing.
Type of hike: A combination of parklike bridges and obscure footpaths. Little or no flagging exists in the upper portion of this hike, but the trail is well worn and the density of wildlife makes it worthwhile.

Elevation gain: No significant elevation gains.
Best season: Year-round.
Land status: The upper segment of this trail falls into the Regional District of Nanaimo's proposed trail corridor. Some segments cross private land. While the current landholder permits trail users, at press time the land was for sale.

Finding the trailhead: Traveling north, follow the Inland Island Highway (19) to the Parksville/Coombs exit. Turn left onto the Port Alberni Highway (4) and left again onto Errington Road. Turn left onto Englishman River Road before you get to Englishman River Provincial Park. Drive to the end and leave your car on the side of the small turnabout. The two entrances to this portion of the trail are not marked but are clearly visible through the trees.

The hike: The hike from the end of Englishman River Road to what locals call "The Nose" begins with a steep drop down to the water's edge followed by a log crossing over Morrison Creek. From here the trail skirts the Englishman River, climbing again to merge with an inactive logging road. When you reach this junction, keep to the right, where the path descends another hill and emerges at the Englishman River Salmon Enhancement Project. A spawning channel and feeding station offer the chance to view coho, chinook, steelhead, and pink salmon on their way to and from the Englishman River. If you hike this portion in May, you may also glimpse heavenly carpets of fawn lily, bleeding heart, and western trillium.

Thanks to hatchery workers, the trail widens at this point, crossing a bridge and following the spawning channel through a bird-watcher's paradise. Black bears and cougars, not to mention people with rottweilers, also frequent this area. Be on the lookout for tracks, particularly during late summer and fall

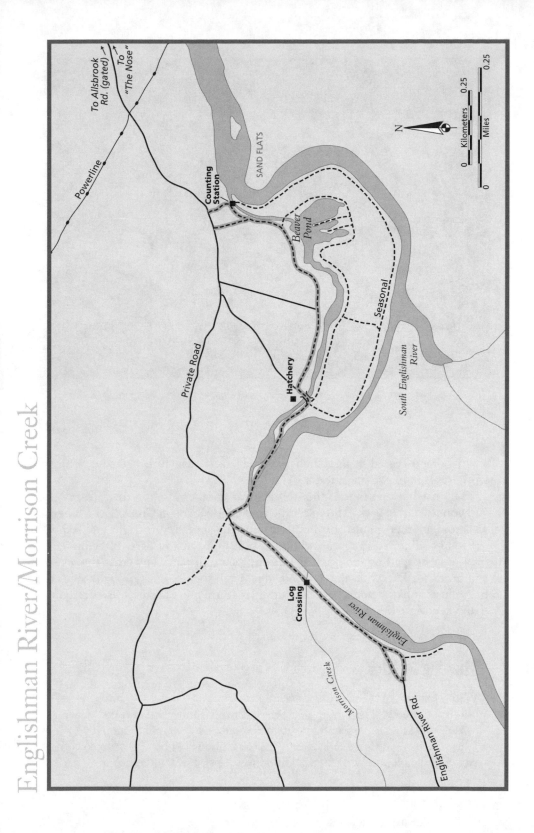

Englishman River/Morrison Creek

Wildflowers abound on Vancouver Island trails—like this bunchberry near Della Falls.

when salmon reared in the hatchery return to spawn. Enhancement project workers also offer seasonal tours.

The hatchery portion of the trail ends at another logging road. Turn left and you will circle back to intersect the trail near Morrison Creek. For a longer walk and another glimpse of the beautiful Englishman, turn right and follow the road to The Nose, a local swimming hole and summer party place marked by a nasal-shaped promontory. While another trail picks up across the water and heads for Parksville along Top Bridge Trail, the presence of highway traffic, industrial parks, and a general glut of cigarette butts makes it less desirable than what came before.

Stinging Nettles

Watch for stinging nettle (*Urtica dioica*) in moist areas around swamps, rivers, ponds, or ditches. The formic acid secreted from hollow hairs on the plant's topside and stem cause painful rashes when encountered unintentionally. This reaction is diffused, however, by several minutes of boiling prior to contact, and the plant makes a nice addition to soups, stews, and omelettes.

Englishman River Falls Provincial Park

A hike along the scenic Englishman River to the upper and lower falls takes less time than your favorite TV show. Take along your family and a picnic and you might just turn that box in for good. (Though there is always room for movies: That stunning canyon beneath the lower bridge is the one featured in Alaska.*) Legend has it that aboriginal peoples discovered the skeleton of a white man on the river near the waterfall. That is why the place is called Englishman River Falls.*

Distance: Approximately 2 kilometers.
Approximate hiking time: 40 minutes.
Difficulty: Easy.
Type of hike: This 97-hectare park offers walking trails through lush forests of Douglas fir, cedar, hemlock, maple, and arbutus.

Elevation gain: No significant elevation gain.
Best season: Year-round. Visitors flock to the park throughout the year for hiking, swimming, and camping, or to see salmon spawning in fall.
Land status: Provincial park.

Finding the trailhead: Traveling north, follow the Inland Island Highway (19) to the Parksville/Coombs exit. Turn left onto the Port Alberni Highway (4) and left again onto Errington Road. Drive to where Errington Road ends at the day-use parking lot in Englishman River Falls Provincial Park. Trails to the upper and lower falls are well marked and can be accessed at two points from the parking lot.

The hike: Englishman River Park is the gem of Errington and boasts a picturesque loop linking two waterfalls. Begin the trail at one of two access points off the parking lot and skirt the falls in half an hour. The main trail crosses the river

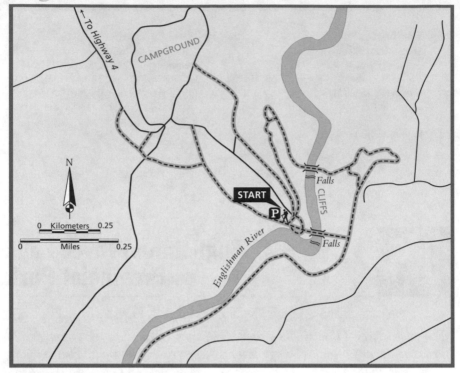

Tidbit

A petroglyph is a design or picture chipped or carved into rock. Some First Nations peoples consider petroglyphs sacred testimonies of their ancestors.

twice. The view from these bridges is breathtaking, as the river crashes down the canyon toward the clear deep pools below the second waterfall. While the upper falls are taller and more spectacular, the lower falls offer good swimming opportunities downstream from the footbridge. A small rocky beach near the lower falls serves as a bird-watching and sunbathing area. Points of interest include a trail that travels upstream from the

The Yew Tree

The western or Pacific yew grows at low to middle elevations in wet areas enriched with abundant soil nutrients. Scientists originally used the tree's bark to manufacture Taxol (a word derived from the *Latin Taxus brevifolia*), a drug used in the treatment of some cancers. Now they breed domestic yews for this purpose.

The Lower Falls of the Englishman River cascade into emerald pools below—a pause here provides a feast for the senses.

upper bridge to a small picnic area. Pit toilets can be found throughout the park, with a flush toilet building located adjacent to the day-use parking lot.

Hike Information

📞 Trail Contact
B.C. Parks: Web site wlapwww.gov.bc.ca/bcparks.

$ Fees/Permits
No fees or permits required. The cost to stay overnight in the park's campground is $15.00 per party from April 1 to October 15, and $8.00 per party from October 16 to March 31.

❓ Local Information
Parksville District Chamber of Commerce, 1275 East Island Highway, Parksville, BC V9P 2G3; phone (250) 248–3613; fax (250) 248–5210; Web site www.chamber.parksville.ca; e-mail info@chamber.parksville.bc.ca.

◆ Maps/Brochures
Englishman River Provincial Park brochure.

16

Little Qualicum Falls Provincial Park

Loop trails on both sides of the Little Qualicum River provide a scenic access to the upper and lower falls. Nearby Cameron Lake Day Use Area also provides great opportunities for swimming: Majestic waterfalls charge down a craggy gorge in a temperate rain forest setting.

Distance: Several kilometers of trails.
Approximate hiking time: 30 to 60 minutes, depending on number of loop trails completed.
Difficulty: Easy.
Type of hike: Easily accessible 440-hectare park with wood steps, gravel and stone paths.

Elevation gain: No significant elevation gain.
Best season: Year-round. On hot summer days the Little Qualicum River Trail offers a shady, refreshing hike through natural, mature, and varied forests.
Land status: Provincial park.

Finding the trailhead: Little Qualicum Falls Provincial Park is located off Highway 4, 19 kilometers from Parksville and 58 kilometers west of Nanaimo. When traveling west, turn right at the sign to the park. Drive along a narrow paved road over railroad tracks and past picnic and campground signs. The road ends at the main parking lot. Both upper and lower falls can be accessed via the main parking lot. You can also park on the left at the smaller parking lot past the campground road. A quick route to the upper falls takes off from this location.

 Brown trout, or *Salmo trutta*, were introduced to North America in 1883 from Europe and western Asia. The Little Qualicum River is one of the few rivers in the province known to have brown trout.

The hike: Little Qualicum Falls Provincial Park incorporates the south shore of Cameron Lake and includes loop trails on both sides of the Little Qualicum River. Surrounded by large stands of mature Douglas fir trees and a rich understory of salal, these trails provide access to two sets of waterfalls. To reach the lower falls, follow the stairs down the path, onto the stone steps, and down onto the Lower Falls Bridge. To reach the upper falls from the main parking lot, follow the signs to the left. Trail maps are located at all path junctions. The park has a ninety-four-campsite campground, two picnic areas, and pit and flush toilets. It is open for walks year-round, though domestic animals must be on leashes at all times.

Options: Little Qualicum Falls Park is also the starting point for a number of longer hikes, including Wesley Ridge and the upstream hike to Cameron Lake. For Wesley Ridge, cross the Upper Falls Bridge and follow an old road straight ahead. This route is a maze of logging roads and spurs and requires maps and know-

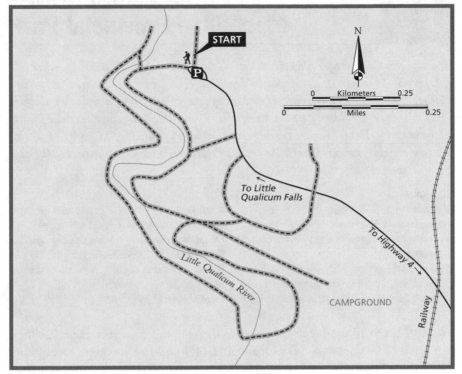

ledge of the area. (See *Hiking Trails II* by the Vancouver Island Trails and Information Society for further details.) Be prepared for logging scars and an uphill climb. For the hike to Cameron Lake, follow an overgrown logging road from the lower campground that leaves the road at the bottom end of the loop. This trail skirts the Little Qualicum River before coming out to the railroad tracks.

Hike Information

Trail Contact
B.C. Parks: Web site
wlapwww.gov.bc.ca/bcparks.

Fees/Permits
No fees or permits required. The cost
to stay overnight in the park's campground is $15.00 per party from April
1 to October 15, and $8.00 per party
from October 16 to March 31.

Local Information
Qualicum Beach Visitor Info Center,
2711 West Island Highway, Qualicum
Beach, BC V9K 2C4; phone (250)
752–9532; fax (250) 752–2923; Web
site www.qualicum.bc.ca; e-mail
info@qualicum.bc.ca.

Maps/Brochures
Little Qualicum Falls Provincial Park
brochure.

Cathedral Grove–
MacMillan Provincial Park

Another great place for families, Cathedral Grove offers short loop trails on either side of Highway 4 through stands of giant old-growth Douglas fir trees, some of which are 800 years old. Mixed with western hemlock, grand fir, and western red cedar, the forest understory is thick with massive ferns, shrubs, and thorny devil's-club. Approximately 750,000 tourists visit the park every year, so please stay on trails. Though the government recently lowered the speed limit through the park, take care when crossing the highway.

Distance: Up to 3 kilometers of short trails.
Approximate hiking time: 30 to 60 minutes, depending on the number of loop trails completed.
Difficulty: Easy.
Type of hike: Easily accessible well-trod paths. If time is an issue, this museumlike forest is a good place to take children (or adults) wanting to learn about Douglas fir, forest ecosystems, tree rings, nurse logs, forest fires, and old-growth trees.
Elevation gain: No significant elevation gains.
Best season: June to September. This park is visited year-round, though back trails can be muddy in the rainy season.
Land status: Provincial park.

Finding the trailhead: Highway 4 runs through this 136-hectare park, which is located 25 kilometers west of Qualicum Beach and 16 kilometers east of Port Alberni on the shores of Cameron Lake. Taking Highway 4 west, the road winds around Cameron Lake to your right. A short ride past the lake takes you past a sign on your left for Cathedral Grove–MacMillan Park. Parking is located on both sides of the highway. Facilities are limited to trails, interpretive signs, outhouses, and a viewing platform. Pets must be leashed.

The hike: The park offers three loops comprised of level boardwalk and dirt path. The main loop is the Big Tree Loop, which is located on the south side of the road. A 1997 storm toppled many old Douglas fir trees in this area. Cedar Tree Loop is on the north side of the road between the highway and

B.C.'s Provincial Tree

The western red cedar, or *Thuja plicata*, is British Columbia's provincial tree. Traditionally First Nations peoples used the tree almost daily, weaving clothes from the cedar's soft inner bark, splitting planks and shingles or forging dugout canoes and totem poles from the tree's trunk. Emily Carr immortalized its long drooping branches in her paintings of West Coast forests, now on display alongside First Nation cedar sculptures, carvings, and masks at the Royal British Columbia Museum.

Cathedral Grove–MacMillan Provincial Park

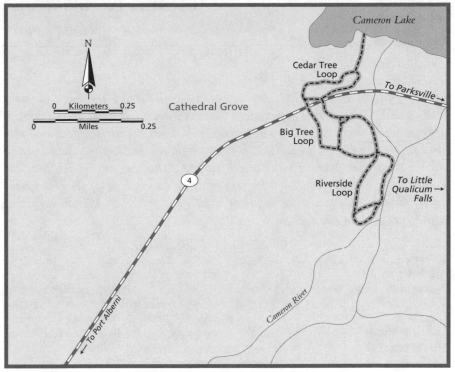

Cameron Lake. This trail winds through groves of ancient western red cedar to the shores of Cameron Lake. Riverside Loop follows Cameron River. Local groups continue to protest logging company plans to log to the park boundary, which, some say, will destroy the wind barrier, creating more blowdowns.

Hike Information

Trail Contact
B.C. Parks: Web site wlapwww.gov.bc. ca/bcparks.

Fees/Permits
No fees or permits required.

Local Information
Qualicum Beach Visitor Info Center, 2711 West Island Highway, Qualicum

Beach, BC V9K 2C4; phone (250) 752–9532; fax (250) 752–2923; Web site www.qualicum.bc.ca; e-mail info@ qualicum.bc.ca.

Maps/Brochures
Cathedral Grove (MacMillan Provincial Park) brochure.

Mount Arrowsmith
Ridge Access Routes

Mount Arrowsmith offers hikers three possible routes to the alpine: Rosseau Trail, the Judge's Route, and Saddle Trail. Because Rosseau Trail parallels the saddle for much of the ascent, offering fewer opportunities for views and wildflowers, this description concentrates on the Judge's Route and Saddle Trail. Rosseau Trail is flagged and takes you onto the west ridge of Mount Cokely. It makes for a longer loop than Saddle Trail. All the trails offer stunning views of neighboring mountains, the Gulf Islands, the Pacific Ocean, and surrounding lakes (among them Emerald Lake). In season, sub-alpine meadows display a rich variety of wildflowers such as red columbine, lilies, daisies, yarrow, and edible thistles.

Distance: Rosseau Trail (2.2 km), Judge's Route (2.5 km), Saddle Trail (2.0 km).

Approximate hiking time: Rosseau Trail (4 hours), Judge's Route (6 hours), Saddle Trail (3 hours).

Difficulty: Moderate to difficult.

Type of hike:

• *Judge's Route:* The Judge's Route is the hardest and longest of the three Mount Arrowsmith climbs. It is also the quickest way to reach the mountain summit. If you want to test your mettle and aren't concerned about the pretty scenery, this route is for you. Although the natural surroundings are still spectacular on this climb, it doesn't compare to Saddle Trail for stunning wildflower meadows.

• *Saddle Trail:* A meandering ascent through second-growth temperate rain forest to subalpine meadows and scrub. Avoid taking shortcuts on the switchbacks. Also avoid picking flowers in the upper meadows.

Elevation gain: Rosseau Trail (600 meters), Judge's Route (1,000 meters), Saddle Trail (450 meters).

Best season: June to September. Alpine hikes mean snow throughout most of the year. Due to tree shelter on this route, snow may linger well into summer.

Land status: Regional park, Crown lands, and Tree Farm License 44 (Weyerhauser).

Judge's Route

Finding the trailhead: Mount Arrowsmith is located off Highway 4 west of Qualicum Beach and east of Port Alberni. Up until recently this mountain was home to a popular ski resort, so the turnoff is clearly marked on the highway. Follow Highway 4 west in the direction of Port Alberni. Turn left off the highway onto a logging road (Summit Main) at the Mount Arrowsmith Ski Hill sign. You are advised to carry chains if traveling these roads in the winter months. Roads are rugged with potholes year-round. Follow the Mount Arrowsmith indication at the fork in the road. Continue on this road (Pass Main) about 2.8 kilometers to the Judge's Route. The Judge's Route starts at the fourth logging road spur heading up Pass Main and is marked at the entrance with a sign. Park your vehicle at the pullout on the side of the road.

Mount Arrowsmith (Ridge Access Routes)

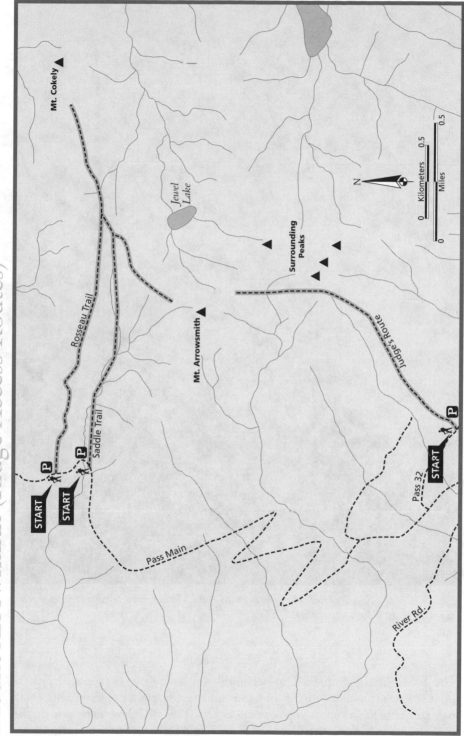

En route to the Saddle Trail, the forested valley by Mount Arrowsmith cradles a sea of mist for an otherworldly view.

The hike: Although this is a nontechnical route requiring no ropes or pickaxes, it is a steady ascent with lots of hands-and-feet scrambling, scree, and, using tree trunks as jungle gyms to pull you forward. This stiff climb takes you up the peak's south side to the first summit, where you'll see an overturned radio tower, or what looks like a green rocket ship. A short climb one level up will bring you to a communications service pipe and wooden platform—a perfect place to rest and eat lunch. This is Mount Arrowsmith's highest peak. At this spot you'll also find a sign-in book. Scribble your name and be proud you made it.

Saddle Trail

Finding the trailhead: This trail begins at a hairpin turn on Pass Main. Follow directions for the Judge's Route above, but instead of parking on Pass Main, continue on up the mountain about 2.8 kilometers past the Judge's Route. Drive (7.3 km) to Pass 37 and park on the side of the road. A white sign marks the trailhead at the end of the road.

The hike: The Saddle Route is located between Mount Cokely and Mount Arrowsmith. Red flagging to the right follows a snaky path that is scattered with tree roots and big rocks. Blue flagging traverses the forest for a less intense uphill climb. If summer conditions have hit the saddle, you can walk up a rocky stream path flanked on either side by a wildflower fringe. This steady ascent to the top takes you to the first wildflower meadow, which—in August— is overflowing with lilies, red columbine, huckleberry, and fireweed. Follow the ridge to the south of the saddle to reach Mount Arrowsmith's main peaks. As you make your way to the subalpine ridges, you will encounter juniper, stunted silver fir, and hemlock, along with various species of lichen. Don't attempt the highest peak (referred to as the "Nose") from this angle without proper mountaineering equipment. A clamber over to the north part of the saddle takes you to the west ridge of Mount Cokely and Rosseau Trail. This vantage point affords a spectacular view of the Pacific Ocean.

Hike Information

Trail Contact
Alpine Club of Canada, B.C. Federation of Mountain Clubs, Peter Rothermel, (250) 752–2529.

Fees/Permits
No fees or permits required.

Local Information
Alberni Valley and Visitor Info Center, R.R. 2, Site 215, C-10, Port Alberni, BC V9Y 7L6; phone (250) 724–6535; fax (250) 724–6560; Web site www.avcoc. com; e-mail avcoc@cedar.alberni.net.

 Maps/Brochures
NTS Map 92 F/7.
Recreation and Logging Road Guide (Weyerhauser).

utes into the trail is a lookout point with a view of pine, yellow cedar, and hemlock trees, along with an out-of-commission ski tow. CPR Trail parallels McBey Creek then veers right. After an hour the trail intersects with a gravel ski road (Pass 40). A short scramble up to this road affords an unimpeded view of the forested valley. Follow this road up the hill until you come to a cross-country ski sign. Turn left to meet M&B Trail.

After about another hour of hiking, a secondary branch will lead you to higher elevations where subalpine brushwood, wild berries (in season), and heather abound. At the top is a series of bog ponds plentiful with bog rosemary, Labrador tea, and crowberry. Follow a five-minute offshoot from this trail to a lookout point with views of Cameron Lake and Vancouver Island to the east. About an hour after the lookout stop, a junction marks the intersection between M&B Trail and Cameron Lake Trail. Take CPR Trail heading back to meet up with McBey Creek and your trail starting point.

Hike Information

 Trail Contact
Alpine Club of Canada, B.C. Federation of Mountain Clubs, Peter Rothermel, (250) 752–2529.

Fees/Permits
No fees or permits required.

 Local Information
Alberni Valley and Visitor Info Center, R.R. 2, Site 215, C-10, Port Alberni, BC V9Y 7L6; phone (250) 724–6535; fax (250) 724–6560; Web site www.avcoc.com; e-mail avcoc@cedar.alberni.net.

Maps/Brochures
NTS Map 92 F/7.
Recreation and Logging Road Guide (Weyerhauser).

Della Falls

At 440 meters, Della Falls is one of the ten largest falls in the world. Access this hike at the west end of Great Central Lake by first renting or chartering a boat and then making your way to the B.C. Parks trailhead. The relatively gentle railway grade follows Drinkwater Creek through deciduous and coniferous forests to a series of stunning waterfalls located in Strathcona Park. The peaks of Big Interior Mountain (1,806 meters), Mount Septimus (1,950 meters), and Nine Peaks (1,842 meters) provide a spectacular addition to the scenery.

Della Falls

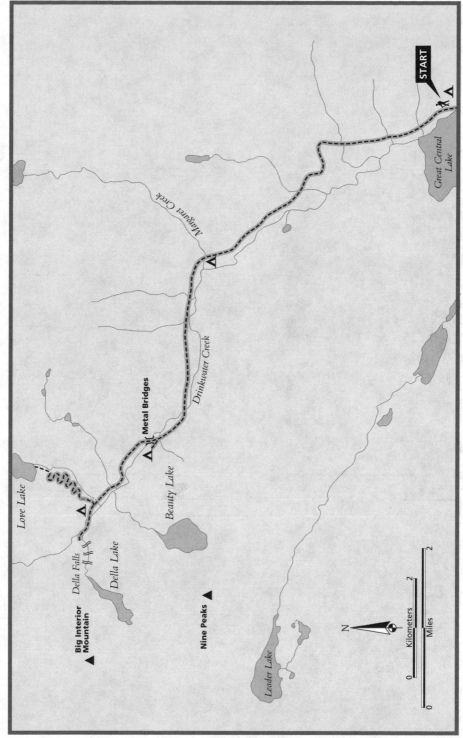

Distance: 16 kilometers.

Approximate hiking time: 5 to 7 hours. If exploring the trail up to Love Lake (4 km one-way), add 2 hours in each direction.

Difficulty: Moderate due to length. The trail to Love Lake is difficult due to steep sections and loose gravel.

Type of hike: Gravel path with some muddy sections and park standard bridges. The trail follows an old railway-logging grade for much of the hike to Della Falls.

Elevation gain: 350 meters. Love Lake is a further 830 meters.

Best season: For Della Falls, June to September. For Love Lake, August to September due to lingering snow at higher elevations.

Land status: Provincial park.

Finding the trailhead: From Port Alberni, follow Highway 4 west for 13 kilometers. Just past Coleman Road, turn right onto Central Lake Road. You will be in the vicinity of Sproat Lake Provincial Park. Follow Central Lake Road for 8 kilometers past the Robertson Creek fish hatchery to where the road meets Great Central Lake. Parking is available for a fee at the Ark Resort, as are canoe and boat rentals. You can also charter a water taxi from the Ark Resort to the Della Falls Trailhead for a somewhat costly per-person fee. If you have your own boat, there is alternate parking at the end of the powerhouse road, the last right before the Ark Resort. Be warned that vandalism occurs with some regularity at this location. To reach this lot, follow the road over the Stamp River Bridge and continue for 6.5 kilometers. Turn left onto Branch 83. After approximately 9 kilometers on Branch 83, turn left onto an unmarked road and travel a further 1.5 kilometers. This location also includes a B.C. forest recreation site.

Great Central Lake is a popular paddling and boating destination and is home to such fish as steelhead, rainbow and cutthroat trout, Dolly Varden, and sockeye salmon. At 5,000 hectares, the lake also presents a considerable paddling challenge with strong winds that have been known to whip the water into nearly 2-meter swells. For those interested in undertaking a complete self-propelled experience, allow up to twelve hours of paddling time one-way. B.C. Parks has provided ample camping space at the Della Falls Trailhead. It is recommended that anyone considering paddling in addition to hiking allow six days in total.

The hike: Della Falls Trail starts at the end of Great Central Lake, just off the B.C. Parks official dock. Here you will find a campsite with outhouse facilities, canoe and kayak racks, and a bearproof food cache. There is also a central group fire ring. The park requests that campers avoid lighting fires in the backcountry unless absolutely necessary. This location was once known as Camp Six and was home to 400 people.

Almost immediately the trail follows a flat wide path through a forest that is mercifully level. This is the beginning of a logging railway built near the turn of the last century to haul precious timbers from the Drinkwater Valley. As you hike, note the abundance of early successional forest characterized by the presence of red alder and big-leaf maple trees. In early summer the light filtering

◀ *Following the trail to Love Lake provides this eye-popping vista of Della Falls.*

through these forests is as breathtaking as any stained-glass window.

Along the trail, the remains of logging and mining activity are also evident. The earliest mining activity started in 1865 when would-be prospectors discovered gold. Chinese placer miners stayed in the area until the 1880s. Watch for the rotting floorboards of an old cabin, weathered log bridges, and, at the Della Falls campsite, rusting saws and the workings of an old mill. Names in the valley also hark back to some early inhabitants. Drinkwater Creek takes its name from Joe Drinkwater, a prospector and trapper from Ontario who christened the penultimate falls in the valley for his wife, Della. He also staked a number of claims, finding gold on the shores of Della Lake and leaving behind buckets, shovels, pipes, and the remains of an aerial tramway and rock crusher when he vacated in 1915.

One impressive feature of this hike is the sheer number of waterfalls. Though Della Falls is certainly the largest and the most impressive of the lot, innumerable creeks empty into the valley from the alpine, cascading over large and small rock faces to join Drinkwater Creek. These creeks provide a cold, clear water source for thirsty hikers, though B.C. Parks still recommends filtering or boiling all drinking water. Parks also requests that you camp in designated areas. Facilities are only available at two locations, but most maps indicate four campsites.

Closer to Della Falls, the forest becomes subalpine with mountain hemlock and yellow cedar popping up more frequently. The only major fork on the Della Falls Trail is at the 15-kilometer mark, just before the Della Falls campsite. Here the trail branches in two directions, heading left to Della Falls and right up and over the ridge to the alpine. The latter route ascends a series of steep switchbacks, crossing small streams via several rotted log bridges before passing over the crown of the ridge. While the Della Falls branch provides a close-up look at the falls, this trail permits a long-range view that includes Della Lake, Beauty Lake, and the three cascades comprising Della Falls. The trail also leads to Love Lake, a chilly aquamarine pool nestled in the grip of Mount Rousseau.

Wildflowers are abundant in most sections of the hike. At lower elevations, particularly the lush open area at the foot of Della Falls, watch for wood violets, bunchberry, bleeding heart, rose-twisted stock, and columbine. At higher elevations, as you ascend the ridge to Love Lake, calypso and coral root orchids

Sproat Lake Provincial Park

For further exploration in the area, visit Sproat Lake Provincial Park, located west of Port Alberni on Sproat Lake. The park offers campsites, swimming, and picnic sites, in addition to First Nations rock carvings known as petroglyphs.

flourish in the rich understory of the forest. In general, wildflowers will be most prolific at lower elevations earlier in summer and at higher elevations later in the season.

Key points (km)

0.0   Start at the B.C. Parks interpretive sign where a map indicates the route to Della Falls and Love Lake.

0.5   The trail passes through early successional forest comprised of big-leaf maple and western hemlock.

2.3   The trail crosses a creek on a single log.

3.8   The trail crosses a creek via a wooden footbridge.

3.9   The trail ascends briefly and then returns to a flat grade.

4.4   The trail crosses another creek.

6.7   Margaret Creek Campsite is located just before the trail veers right.

6.9   The trail ascends after the Margaret Creek Bridge.

7.1   The trail descends and returns to the railway grade. Watch for wild ginger growing low to the ground.

8.5   The trail crosses another creek.

9.4   The trail crosses a wooden footbridge over a creek.

10.6   Artifacts from an old railway are evident to your left.

11.5   The trail crosses Drinkwater Creek via a wooden trestle. Watch for views of Big Interior Mountain and creek rapids.

12.8   The trail forks. For Good Camp, turn left and follow the trail over rock slides and through alders for approximately 200 meters. This campsite may be flooded at certain times of year. For Della Falls, follow the main trail to the right across two metal bridges spanning Drinkwater Creek.

13.2   The trail follows alongside Drinkwater Creek across streamside boulders.

14.0   The trail returns to a level grade.

14.2   The trail follows a wooden bridge across a creek. Look to your right for an impressive cascade.

15.0   The trail to Love Lake and Mount Rousseau veers right. Head left for Della Falls.

15.5   The trail reaches Della Falls main base camp. At the far edge of camp, a scenic gorge overlooks the creek.

15.8   The trail passes through an open area where wildflowers and shrubs are abundant.

16.2   The trail reaches Della Falls. Near the base of the falls, artifacts from mining and logging activity lie rusting in the undergrowth.

Hike Information

Trail Contacts

B.C. Parks: Web site wlapwww.gov.bc. ca/bcparks.
Ark Resort, 11000 Great Central Lake Road, Site 306 C-1, R.R. 3, Port Alberni, BC V9Y 7L7; phone/fax (250) 723–2657; Web site arkresort.com; e-mail admin@ArkResort.com.

Fees/Permits

No fees or permits required.

Local Information

Alberni Valley and Visitor Info Center, R.R. 2, Site 215, C-10, Port Alberni, BC V9Y 7L6; phone (250) 724–6535; fax (250) 724–6560; Web site www.avcoc. com; e-mail avcoc@cedar.alberni.net.

Maps/Brochures

NTS Maps 92 F/5, 92 F/6.
Strathcona Provincial Park brochure.
Ark Resort trail map.

21

Alone Mountain

This steep, half-day climb over forested and rocky terrain culminates in views of Comox Lake and the Cruickshank River. Hike this trail in early to midsummer and you may catch vivid displays of alpine and subalpine wildflowers such as harebells and lupines. At lower elevations watch for killdeer nesting on bare rock faces, in addition to rare displays of Pacific dogwood, coral root orchids, and nodding onions. This trail is located off Comox Lake Main south of Strathcona Park and requires a short drive on rough roads.

Distance: Approximately 3 kilometers.
Approximate hiking time: 2½ hours.
Difficulty: Difficult with moderate sections.
Type of hike: Isolated but well marked.

Elevation gain: Approximately 600 meters.
Best season: June to October.
Land status: Crown land and Tree Farm License (TimberWest Forest Products).

Finding the trailhead: From Cumberland, take Fourth Street to Bevan Road. Follow Bevan Road to the stop sign and set your odometer at zero. Turn left onto Comox Lake Main, also known as Colake Main, and drive for 16.3 kilometers, passing the Courtenay Fish and Game Association and the Comox Dam Recreation Area. The road is drivable but rough, with single-lane bridges and frequent logging trucks. Check with TimberWest for logging activity and road conditions. The trailhead is the next gravel road on the right past branch 2700, and is marked EMERGENCY HELIPORT/ALONE MOUNTAIN TRAILHEAD. Park in the pullout and walk up the gravel road until it ends at an open lot. Follow

Alone Mountain

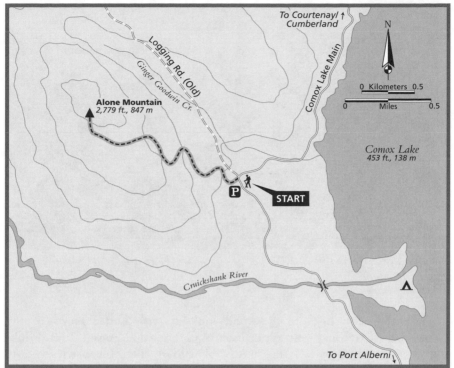

the tree line to your right where flagging tape and orange tags mark the trail.

The hike: The Alone Mountain Trail begins with low-canopy forest of immature Douglas fir leading down to a creek. As you begin to climb, the forest matures with large examples of western red cedar and Pacific dogwood, British Columbia's provincial flower.

The first lookout provides views of Comox Lake and the Cruickshank River to the left as you ascend, and the Comox Valley to the right. After this lookout the forest matures considerably, winding through mossy glades and lichen-covered cliffs. After approximately an hour, the trail moves over moss-covered boulders and turns sharply up the mountain to follow a series of switchbacks. Be prepared for a steep ascent and some hiking on bare rock.

 Because the blooms of the Pacific dogwood (*Cornus nuttalii*) are the floral emblems of British Columbia, a law prohibiting the cutting down or digging up of these trees is in place.

For this picture-perfect view of Comox Lake, stop at the first lookout on your way up Alone Mountain.

The trail continues to a second lookout with better views of the Cruickshank River and west to the Strait of Georgia and Powell River. If hiking in late summer or early fall, watch for wild creeping blueberries, a tasty addition to a quick break. Although this is one of the finest views on Alone Mountain, the trail continues along the ridge in a gradual ascent for another half an hour. The benefits of hiking the final portion of the trail include glimpses of alpine wildflowers and views to the west.

Hike Information

Trail Contact/Local Information
Cumberland Visitor Information Center, P. O. Box 250, Cumberland, BC V0R 1S0; phone (250) 336–8313; fax (250) 336–2455; Web site www.island. net/~cumbcham; e-mail cumbcham@ island.net.

Road Information
TimberWest Forest Information Office, #3–4890 Rutherford Road, Nanaimo, BC V9T 4Z4; phone (250) 729–3766.

Fees/Permits
No fees or permits required.

Maps/Brochures
NTS Map 92 F/11.
District Map of the Comox Valley and Surrounding Area (Comox Valley Search and Rescue Association).
Logging and Highway Road Map, Buttle/Comox Lake to Sayward (Campbell River Search and Rescue Society).

Puntledge River Trail

This low-elevation mixed-use trail follows the Puntledge River from several access points and offers hikes from twenty minutes to a full day. Opportunities are available to link up with the trail system in Nymph Falls Regional Park farther downstream, as well as Nymph Falls, the Comox Dam Recreation Area, and some lovely swimming holes. Although these trails carry the obvious mark of hydroelectric activity, they are also fine opportunities to explore both sides of the river. In the event of rising water levels, sirens will sound, indicating evacuation of the river channel. The trails are currently being upgraded to accommodate multiple uses.

Distance: Up to 20 kilometers of trail with various access points.
Difficulty: Easy.
Type of hike: Well-maintained popular gravel trail with sections of boardwalk.
Elevation gain: No significant elevation gains.
Best season: Mid-April to October.
Land status: B.C. Hydro lands and regional park.

Finding the trailhead: From Cumberland, follow Bevan Road until Comox Lake Main. Turn left and drive to the Comox Dam, which signals entry points on both sides of the river. From Courtenay, follow Forbidden Plateau Road to Upper Puntledge Hatchery Road and park outside the Upper Puntledge Hatchery. All trailheads are marked with color maps and wooden trail signs.

The hike: On the east side of the river, follow the flat gravel trail through sections of mixed forest, peat bog, and mature Douglas fir. The easy walking continues the full length of the trail with many hewn log benches and swimming areas, and links up with a footpath to the Bevan Hostel. For views to Nymph Falls, follow the trail to a gravel road that turns left and crosses the B.C. Hydro pipeline ending at the river. The main branch of the trail continues along the pipeline as a gravel road for another 4 kilometers.

On the northwest side of the river, follow the mixed-use trail through mature and new forests or around Twin Lakes Loop. This side of the trail links up with Nymph Falls Regional Park and further trails to the picturesque Nymph Falls. This trail also leads to the Upper Puntledge Hatchery, accessible via Upper Puntledge Hatchery Road. Although most of the trail is narrow

Tidbit While most alders are shrubs, the red alder *(Alnus rubra)* is a coastal tree that enriches early successional forests with much-needed nitrogen. Locals often employ alder chips when smoking meat and fish. Watch for red alder alongside creeks and rivers.

Puntledge River Trail

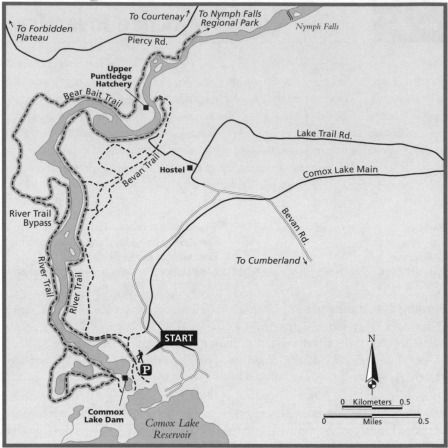

gravel, some sections follow roadways. B.C. Hydro sources indicate future plans to install a suspension bridge for a northeast river crossing.

Options: Nymph Falls is a fifty-three-hectare regional park accessible via the northwest side of the Puntledge River Trail. While the Long and Short Loop Trails are pedestrian only, be prepared to share the other trails with bikers.

Hike Information

Trail Contact
Community Interests Management,
B.C. Hydro, 6911 Southpoint Drive
(E8), Burnaby, BC V3N 4X8; phone
(604) 528–7815.

Fees/Permits
No fees or permits required.

Local Information
Comox Valley Chamber of Commerce,
2040 Cliffe Avenue, Courtenay, BC V9N
2L3; phone (250) 334–3234; fax
(250) 334–4908; Web site www.
tourism-comox-valley.bc.ca; e-mail

chamber@mars.ark.com.
**Cumberland Visitor Information
Center,** P. O. Box 250, Cumberland, BC
V0R 1S0; phone (250) 336–8313; fax
(250) 336–2455; Web site www.island.
net/~cumbcham; e-mail cumbcham@
island.net.

Maps/Brochures
NTS Map 92 F/11.
**District Map of the Comox Valley and
Surrounding Area** (Comox Valley
Search and Rescue Association).
Nymph Falls Regional Nature Park
brochure.

23

Boston Ridge/Mount Becher

Often tricky to locate, this trail can be hiked as two separate ascents or as one full-day loop. Located near the old Forbidden Plateau ski lodge, this steep hike passes through mixed forest to panoramic views of Comox Lake and the Comox Valley. For those agile enough to cross slippery logjams and descend embankments using knotted ropes, this hike includes rewards such as a waterfall on the Boston River and linkages to Forbidden Plateau trails within Strathcona Park.

Distance: 13-kilometer loop.
Approximate hiking time: 8 hours.
Difficulty: Moderate with difficult sections. The Boston Ridge trail includes a slippery crossing over a logjam.

Type of hike: Forest path with near-miss markings.
Elevation gain: 580 meters.
Best season: June to September.
Land status: Crown lands and provincial park.

Finding the trailhead: From the Inland Island Highway, take exit 127 (Forbidden Plateau Recreation Area), which is marked as Piercy Road. Turn right onto Forbidden Plateau Road and follow the loop as it crosses back over the highway. After the road changes to gravel, continue up the mountain over a series of switchbacks until you see a sign indicating Mount Becher/Boston Ridge. The sign is easy to miss and is posted immediately before the private chalet-style settlements. If you reach the old Forbidden Plateau Ski Lodge,

Boston Ridge/Mount Becher

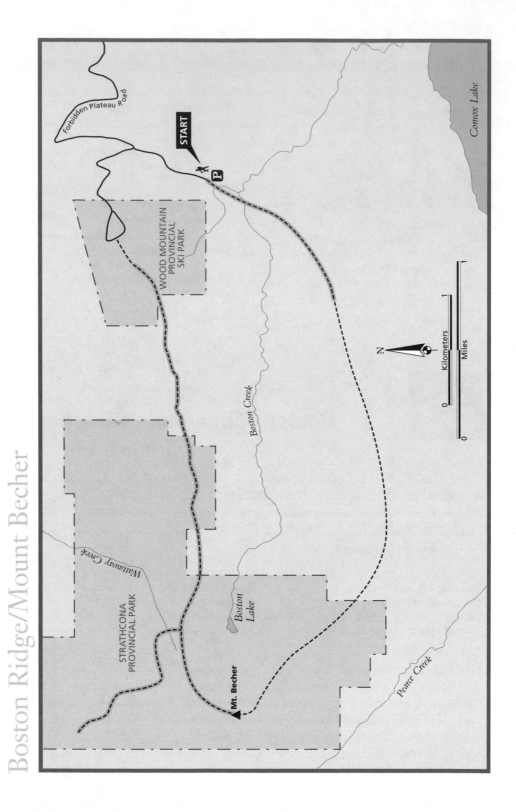

you have gone too far. Park at the sign where the road widens considerably and walk down the old road to your left. This road ends at a trio of paths leading off into the forest and up the mountain. (An alternate route to Mount Becher involves ascending the steep path on your right and watching for signs indicating the trailhead.) For Boston Ridge, walk straight ahead and watch for a small sign attached to a tree. Boston Ridge Trail begins by following the Boston River.

The hike: Follow the forest path down to the creek, where big-leaf maples flank the trail. An initial crossing over a small stream may require waterproof shoes in early spring. Once on the other side, follow the path to where it meets the river a second time. This tricky crossing involves a sharp descent via a rough rope, a short ladder ending in a pool of water, and a slippery logjam. The crossing is considerably easier during low water. Also keep in mind that water levels rise quickly during wet weather and may cut off eager hikers in the case of flash floods. The first waterfall is visible upstream from the midpoint of the crossing.

The ascent of the ridge begins on the other side of the river. Follow the path, flagged now by red stakes driven in the ground and metallic tree markers, through forest dominated by Douglas fir, hemlock, and cedar. The climax of this hike is an opening in the trees that affords views of Comox Lake and the Comox Valley. Active logging may not be far away, so be prepared for clear-cuts and farm-style forest views. To complete the entire loop, continue hiking via the Mount Becher summit, where you can connect with Strathcona Provincial Park trails. The main trail will take you down to the Forbidden Plateau Ski Lodge, where you can hook up with the road and walk back to your car.

Options: To begin with Mount Becher, ascend the mountain path from the old ski lodge following blazes up the ski run. Pass under the T bar to the Mount Becher Trailhead for views of the Comox Valley, the Strait of Georgia, and a panorama of the Coast Mountains on the B.C. mainland.

Hike Information

Trail Contact
B.C. Parks: Web site wlapwww.gov.bc.ca/bcparks.

Fees/Permits
No fees or permits required.

Local Information
Comox Valley Chamber of Commerce, 2040 Cliffe Avenue, Courtenay, BC V9N

2L3; phone (250) 334–3234; fax (250) 334–4908; Web site www.tourism-comox-valley.bc.ca; e-mail chamber@mars.ark.com.

 Maps/Brochures
NTS Map 92 F/11.
Strathcona Provincial Park brochure.
Forbidden Plateau map (B.C. Parks).

Forbidden Plateau

Access to the alpine has never been easier. This moderate hike starting from Mount Washington Alpine Resort moves through subalpine forests and meadows to a series of lakes and scenic viewpoints. Two interconnected loops offer day-hiking possibilities, while trails above Lake Helen Mackenzie lead to numerous alpine and subalpine overnight destinations. These trails also provide access to an extensive set of hiking routes, including those leading to Mount Albert Edward, Castlecrag Mountain, and Moat Lake. This hike is full of superlatives, including glacier-fed lakes, snowcapped mountains, ice fields, and stunning views of surrounding mountain ranges from Mount Albert Edward and Cruickshank Canyon.

Distances and Approximate Hiking Times:
- *Paradise Meadows Loop:* 3 kilometers—45 minutes.
- *Helen Mackenzie/Battleship Lake Loop:* 6.8 kilometers—2½ hours.
- *Paradise Meadows Trailhead to Kwai Lake:* 7 kilometers—3 hours.
- *Paradise Meadows Trailhead to Canyon Lookout:* 8.5 kilometers—4 hours.
- *Paradise Meadows Trailhead to Circlet Lake:* 10 kilometers—4 hours.
- *Circlet Lake to Mount Albert Edward Summit:* 6 kilometers—4 hours.

Difficulty: To Circlet Lake the trail remains easy to moderate. After Circlet Lake, the trail rises sharply and crosses a number of bare rock sections requiring confident footwork.

Type of hike: The trail is a well-used bark mulch path and boardwalk up to Lake Helen Mackenzie, including park standard bridges and campsites. After Lake Helen Mackenzie, the trail changes to a well-marked bare ground path that has a tendency to get muddy in spring and fall. Rock cairns erected by hikers mark routes above the tree line.

Elevation gain:
- *Paradise Meadows Trailhead to Kwai Lake:* 250 meters.
- *Circlet Lake to Mount Albert Edward summit:* 900 meters.

Best season: August to September. Forbidden Plateau is also a popular location for snowshoeing, backcountry skiing, and winter camping.

Land status: Provincial park.

Finding the trailhead: From Nanaimo, take the Inland Island Highway north. Follow the exit to Mount Washington via the Strathcona Parkway for 25 kilometers. Turn left onto Nordic Lodge Road and drive for approximately 1.5 kilometers to the Paradise Meadows parking lot. This is also the old Mount Washington Nordic Lodge parking lot. The trailhead is located slightly below the brow of the hill. You can also access Forbidden Plateau via the old Forbidden Plateau Ski Area and Wood Mountain Provincial Park. That entry point does not provide direct access to the trails described here.

The hike(s): Paradise Meadows Loop: From the trailhead, follow a gravel trail down to Paradise Meadows where you will see the beginning of the boardwalk. Taking the first or second left that you encounter will keep you on the Paradise

Forbidden Plateau

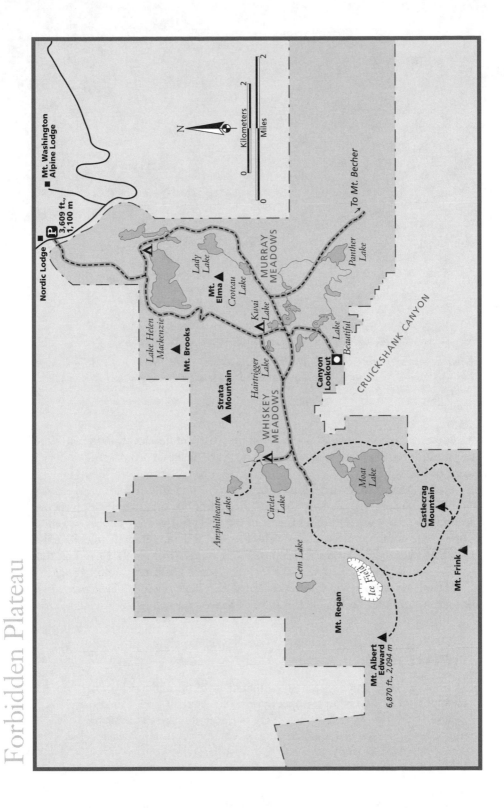

Wide boardwalks protect fragile wildflower meadows on the first leg of the Forbidden Plateau hike. This return view shows a popular Mount Washington ski run in the distance.

Meadows section of the trail, leading you through middle-elevation forest. Here the meadows are replete with wildflowers, berry bushes, cotton grass, and sections of low-lying fen.

Helen Mackenzie/Battleship Lake Loop: From the Paradise Meadows Trailhead, stay on the boardwalk past the first turnoff and follow the loop via the second left or straight ahead. This part of the trail leads you up a series of gentle slopes, into forest punctuated by yellow cedar and mountain hemlock. Lake Helen Mackenzie, the largest lake on this trail, offers a camping area and pit toilets. Mountains overlooking the lake include Mount Elma and Mount Brooks.

Helen Mackenzie to Circlet Lake: After Lake Helen Mackenzie, two branches of trail lead on to Circlet Lake. The west branch passes through dark,

Whiskey Jacks

Whiskey jacks or gray jays are bold inhabitants of the alpine who will often swoop down to land in an open palm or on the edge of a boot to get at snacks. They are omnivorous—feeding on meat, insects, and available fruit—and will appropriate just about anything. Their *whee-ah, chuck-chuck* call is a signal that they are in the area and will soon be paying you a visit.

mature forest and skirts the edge of Hairtrigger Lake. On this route you have the option of bypassing Kwai Lake and heading directly for Whiskey Meadows. During the summer you may also stop at the ranger cabin located before Hairtrigger Lake for information on the park and trail conditions. The east branch starts from Battleship

Lake and passes Kooso, Lady, and Croteau Lakes before traversing Murray Meadows. Although this route may be slightly longer, depending on your destination, it is also the most scenic. Passing by the Kwai Lake campsites, the east branch offers views of Castlecrag Mountain and Mariwood Lake. The branch also gives you the option of a side trip to Cruickshank Canyon Lookout, one of the nicest viewpoints on the official trail system, which passes Lake Beautiful, low waterfalls, and an alpine moonscape dotted with wild blueberries. Looking down the canyon on a clear day, you will see the Cruickshank River rushing on to Comox Lake.

If stopping overnight at Kwai, Helen Mackenzie, or Circlet Lakes—the designated camping areas on the plateau—be prepared to boil or filter your water. B.C. Parks suggests this precaution for all areas of the park. An informative display listing campsite rules is also posted at all campgrounds. Amenities include pit toilets, gray water disposal, and food caches to protect your food from bears. Some campsites at Kwai Lake afford a stunning view of Mariwood Lake and surrounding peaks.

At Whiskey Meadows, the two main branches of trail converge and follow a series of open grassy areas over boardwalk and bedrock to the end of the trail. A right branch leads to campsites on Circlet Lake and, beyond, to Amphitheatre Lake. The former is a popular camping area for those planning to hike Mount Albert Edward and other nearby routes. Watch for wildflowers in season, including lupine, aster, heather, and arnica.

Circlet Lake to Mount Albert Edward: Ascending the summit of Mount Albert Edward requires a full day of steady hiking, in addition to a topographic map and compass. After leaving Circlet Lake, follow trail markers leading southwest. Almost immediately the trail ascends sharply through uniform forest, then heads straight up the bluff. Once you have mounted the first ridge, flagging tape marks several routes to the summit. The most straightforward (and perhaps the steepest) ascends to the left over a staircase of rock and scree. From this point on rock cairns are the only markers, and you must rely on your orienteering skills to find the ice field. Depending on your approach (and the weather), the summit may not be visible until you are within several kilometers of the top. The final climb to the ice field is over a loose boulder surface and offers gorgeous views in all directions. From the ice field, the peak is a gradual ascent along a sloping ridge to 2,093 meters.

Hike Information

☎ Trail Contact
B.C. Parks: Web site
wlapwww.gov.bc.ca/bcparks.

$ Fees/Permits
An overnight backcountry camping fee
of $5.00 per person, per night is
required for overnight stays. There are
forty-four backcountry sites on
Forbidden Plateau.

❓ Local Information
Comox Valley Chamber of Commerce,
2040 Cliffe Avenue, Courtenay, BC V9N
2L3; phone (250) 334–3234; fax
(250) 334–4908; Web site www.
tourism-comox-valley.bc.ca; e-mail
chamber@mars.ark.com.

Ⓐ Maps/Brochures
NTS Map 92 F/11.
Strathcona Provincial Park brochure.
Forbidden Plateau map (B.C. Parks).

25 Elk Falls Provincial Park

Located just outside the town of Campbell River, this picturesque trail series meanders along the Campbell and Quinsam Rivers through popular fly-fishing areas. Waterfalls, beaver ponds, salmon enhancement spawning channels, and various viewpoints along the Campbell and Quinsam Rivers are just some of the highlights of this gentle nature walk. While the bulk of these trails are located within Elk Falls Provincial Park, access via the John Hart Generating Station provides another alternative to extend your walk. Be prepared for the sights and sounds of hydroelectric activity.

Distance: Up to 6 kilometers.
Approximate hiking time: An easy half day.
Difficulty: Easy.
Type of hike: Well-marked nature trail.
Elevation gain: No significant elevation gain.

Best season: Year-round, although campground services are provided only May 1 to September 31. During the winter and spring seasons, Elk Falls is a more impressive cascade due to higher water levels.
Land status: Provincial park.

Finding the trailhead: Follow Highway 28 north from Campbell River approximately 3 kilometers. Park at any one of three signed trailheads accessing Elk Falls Provincial Park, including one at the John Hart Generating Station (operated by B.C. Hydro) marked as Canyon View Trail.

The hike: Elk Falls Provincial Park offers a number of easy loops along the Campbell and Quinsam Rivers through mixed semimature forest. If you begin

Elk Falls Provincial Park

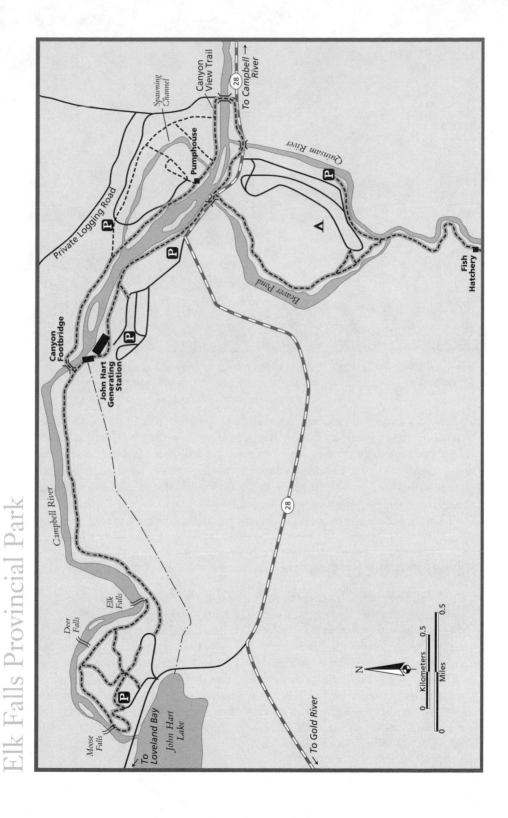

The trail through Elk Falls Provincial Park leads to several lookouts along the Elk River. Stop at this viewpoint to watch the river tumble swiftly toward the falls.

at the B.C. Hydro entrance, you will first skirt the John Hart Generating Station before crossing an impressive canyon to view the river below. Follow this northernmost branch of trail east and you will link up with gravel trails along Department of Fisheries salmon spawning areas. These human-made channels offer interpretive displays on the life cycles of various salmonids and, seasonally, the chance to view spawning salmon.

Turn left before the canyon bridge and you will encounter the westernmost

Swim with the Salmon

Each fall, when salmon return to the Campbell and Quinsam Rivers to spawn, people don snorkels, wet suits, and masks and hop into the cold waters hoping to swim with the salmon. While this chilly experience is one way to get back to nature, some rules do apply. Fisheries officials ask that swimmers enter below the Quinsam and take care not to disturb salmon digging in the gravel. Snorkelers also find that drifting along like a hapless stick affords better opportunities for blending in. Several companies in the town of Campbell River now provide guided swims as well as equipment rentals. Contact the Campbell River Tourist Information Center for more information on this seasonal adventure.

The following nature walks and short hikes offer opportunities for those with limited physical ability and time to view the varying landscapes of Strathcona Park. All trails are well-defined, low-elevation hikes that can be accessed through the main entry portal of the park, located just off Highway 28.

Karst Creek

Distance: 2 kilometers. Approximate hiking time: 40 minutes.

Trail summary: The trail begins with a quick wander through a recent burn. This area provides an example of forest regeneration, and leads to the appearing and disappearing creeks characteristic of limestone wonderlands. Following this section, the trail passes through mature forest to the Karst Creek waterfall, a picturesque cascade surrounded by western red cedar and steep cliffs.

Shepherd's Creek

Distance: 2 kilometers. Approximate hiking time: 40 minutes.

Trail summary: Find the trailhead for Shepherd's Creek across the road from the Ralph River Campground. The trail skirts the river for approximately 200 meters before ascending over a series of gentle switchbacks through a virgin watershed. A marshy area complete with reedy ponds and lily pads is the highlight of this brief but scenic walk.

Lady Falls

Distance: 900 meters. Approximate hiking time: 20 minutes.

Trail summary: Access the trail via Highway 28 approximately 10 kilometers after the east portal. The trail includes a viewing platform and the clear running water of Lady Falls.

Wild Ginger

Distance: 1 kilometer. Approximate hiking time: 20 minutes.

Trail summary: The trail begins just north of the Ralph River Campground entrance on the opposite side of Western Mines Road. Follow the path through a short loop that includes mature forests, wildflowers, and the trail's namesake, the coarse-leafed wild ginger plant, which grows along the ground.

Myra Falls

Distance: 1 kilometer. Approximate hiking time: 20 minutes.

Trail summary: Not to be confused with Upper Myra Falls, this trail begins at the foot of Buttle Lake where Western Mines Road begins to climb. The falls are at the mouth of Myra Creek on a trail that includes a steep hill with loose rock.

Tidbit

Fragments of crinoids, or ancient sea lilies, are the most common fossils found in Strathcona Park. They are ancient relatives of modern-day sea stars and sea cucumbers.

loop of trail skirting three cascades, including 25-meter Elk Falls, and slightly more challenging terrain. Viewers of the falls will see more impressive water levels in winter and spring months.

The southernmost branch of trail, accessible via Highway 28 and the southern portion of Canyon View Trail, leads to the Quinsam River Fish Hatchery along a beaver pond and the picturesque Kingfisher Trail. View steelhead in the Quinsam between November and March. There is also a provincial campground in this section of the park with 122 sites.

Hike Information

Trail Contacts
B.C. Parks: Web site
wlapwww.gov.bc.ca/bcparks.

Fees/Permits
Overnight fees apply when staying in the Elk Falls campground. From May 1 to September 30, fees are $12.00 per party, per night. From October 1 to April 31, fees are $8.00 per party, per night.

Local Information
Campbell River Visitor Info Center,
1235 Shoppers Way, Campbell River, BC V9W 5B6; phone (250) 287–4636; fax (250) 286–6948; Web site www.campbellriverchamber.ca; e-mail visitorinfo@campbellriverchamber.ca.

26

Crest Mountain

A favorite spot for climbers, Crest Mountain is also a breathtaking hike to gorgeous views of Strathcona's snowcapped wonderland from 1,500-plus meters. This steep climb winds its way straight up the mountain in places, offering a quick transition from forest to alpine. Views include glimpses of King's Peak, Puzzle Mountain, and the Elk River Valley. Though this is one of the few alpine hikes in the park that does not lead to further ridge routes, there is a camping area at 1,400 meters adjacent to an unnamed lake.

Crest Mountain

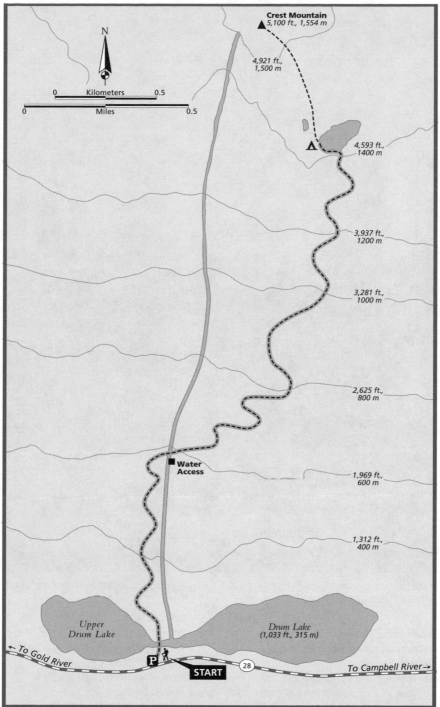

N

0 Kilometers 0.5

0 Miles 0.5

Crest Mountain
▲ 5,100 ft., 1,554 m

4,921 ft.,
1,500 m

Δ 4,593 ft.,
1400 m

3,937 ft.,
1200 m

3,281 ft.,
1000 m

2,625 ft.,
800 m

■ **Water
Access**

1,969 ft.,
600 m

1,312 ft.,
400 m

*Upper
Drum Lake*

*Drum Lake
(1,033 ft., 315 m)*

← To Gold River

P

START   28   To Campbell River →

In addition to stunning views, the landscape atop Crest Mountain offers crystal clear pools and mountain heather.

Distance: 5.5 kilometers.

Approximate hiking time: 3 to 4 hours.

Difficulty: Difficult.

Type of hike: A steep climb over switchbacks and straightaways with some loose-surface and bare rock scrambling. Once over the ridge, an unofficial route to Crest Mountain is marked by rock cairns and a braided pathway through the heather.

Elevation gain: 1,250 meters.

Best season: August to September.

Land status: Provincial park.

Finding the trailhead: From Campbell River, follow Highway 28 west to Strathcona Park. The Crest Mountain Trailhead is located on the right, approximately 20 kilometers from the Buttle Lake Campground.

The hike: From the trailhead, Crest Mountain Trail passes through young alder forest, and then over a bridge between Upper Drum and Drum Lakes. Drum Lake is at elevation 315 meters, which means the trail climbs 1,250 meters in just over 5.5 kilometers. The bulk of elevation is gained in the first 3 kilometers, however, making for a steep trail that waggles its way straight up the mountain.

There is only one place to obtain water between the parking area and the top of the ridge. Access the creek where a bridge made from a fallen cedar spans the crossing. After this crossing, the trail leads you away from the creek, ascending steeply through forest dominated by Douglas fir and western red cedar. Changes in elevation are marked by the presence of yellow cedar, amabilis fir, and mountain hemlock. The first spectacular views of the hike can be had as the trail leaves the dense forest and meets the rocky surface of mountain cliffs.

Once above the ridge, the trail ends at an unnamed glacial lake that marks a potential camping area. Further exploration to the west of the lake reveals a number of unofficial routes to Crest Mountain's peak. Follow these along the ridge through sparse mountain hemlock, heather, and various alpine wildflowers, including aster, arnica, and penstemmon. Views from the ridge include the Elk River Valley, Puzzle Mountain, and King's Peak to the south, and Mount Heber and the Heber Valley to the west. This is one of the few alpine hikes in Strathcona that does not link to further ridge routes.

Hike Information

⬤ Trail Contact
B.C. Parks: Web site wlapwww.gov.bc.ca/bcparks.

$ Fees/Permits
An overnight backcountry camping fee of $5.00 per person, per night is required for overnight stays.

? Local Information
Campbell River Visitor Info Center,
P. O. Box 400, 1235 Shoppers Row,

Campbell River, BC V9W 5B6; toll-free (800) 463–4386; phone (250) 287–4636; Web site www.campbellriver chamber.ca; e-mail visitorinfo@camp bellriverchamber.ca.

▲ Maps/Brochures
NTS Map 92 F/13.
Strathcona Provincial Park brochure.

Elk River Trail/Landslide Lake

For a gentle wilderness backcountry hike, follow this trail along the lush Elk River Valley and visit a glacial lake surrounded by snowcapped peaks. In addition to mature hemlock forests, the hike also boasts abundant waterfalls and several backcountry camping options for overnight stays. Elk River Trail gets its name from the rare and beautiful Roosevelt elk that make their home in the valley.

Distance: 11 kilometers.
Approximate hiking times:
• *To Landslide Lake*—4 to 6 hours.
• *To Iceberg Lake*—6 to 8 hours.
Difficulty: The hike to Landslide Lake is easy with moderate sections. Beyond Landslide Lake the hike follows a rough route.
Type of hike: A forest trail ascending to a bedrock path. This hike is well flagged and well maintained with park standard bridges, outhouses, and food caches at both designated campsites. Despite what the maps say, campsite number one is just before Butterwort Creek at kilometer 6. The upper Gravel Bar campsite is at kilometer 9.
Elevation gain: 550 meters.
Best season: June to August. Be sure to check with B.C. Parks if you do not wish to encounter snow at the upper end of the trail. Muddy patches may also exist earlier in the season.
Land status: Provincial park.

Finding the trailhead: Follow Highway 28 west from Campbell River toward Gold River. After the Strathcona Park entry portal, continue on 28 past Western Mines Road. If you need information on trail conditions or other updates, take a brief detour down Western Mines Road and speak to the volunteers or staff at park headquarters. Once back on Highway 28, a provincial park sign marks the Elk River Trailhead. Purchase your backcountry camping pass from the self-service dispensers if you plan to stay overnight.

The hike: Elk River Trail is a good standby for rainy weather or an early-summer hike since much of the trail is at low elevation and under the cover of mature hemlock forest. Hike this trail in the rain, however, and you may miss the spectacular vantage point at Landslide Lake where fog has a tendency to sock in Mount Colonel Foster and adjacent peaks. (If this does happen, wait a few minutes. Clouds move quickly in these mountains.) If you have a proper water filter, the abundance of mineral-slaked creeks and streams makes the added burden of carrying water unnecessary. Take one bottle and filter as you go. Short of ice, this water is as cold as it comes. Shorter day hikes can also be had along the trail to Butterwort Falls or the cliffs of Elkhorn Mountain, while longer, unofficial routes crisscross the area behind Landslide Lake, leading to Burman Lake and the Golden Hinde. To reap the rewards of Landslide and Iceberg Lakes, the focus of this hike, one or two nights may be necessary.

Elk River Trail begins as a level path and passes immediately through forest dominated by mature Douglas fir. Soon after, the trail makes its first ascent up the

Elk River Trail/Landslide Lake

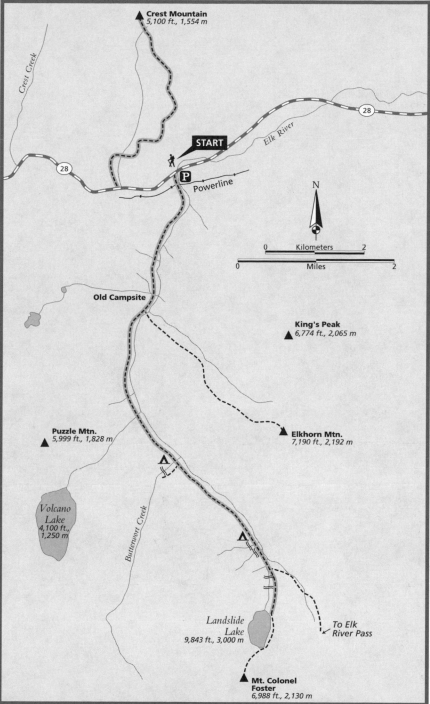

Crest Mountain
5,100 ft., 1,554 m

Crest Creek

28

START

Elk River

P

Powerline

N

| 0 | Kilometers | 2 |

| 0 | Miles | 2 |

28

Old Campsite

King's Peak
▲ *6,774 ft., 2,065 m*

Puzzle Mtn.
▲ *5,999 ft., 1,828 m*

Elkhorn Mtn.
▲ *7,190 ft., 2,192 m*

Butterwort Creek

Volcano Lake
4,100 ft., 1,250 m

Landslide Lake
9,843 ft., 3,000 m

To Elk River Pass

▲ **Mt. Colonel Foster**
6,988 ft., 2,130 m

ridge over a series of gentle switchbacks, then down into the Elk River Valley, where it remains level and follows the river to the first campsite.

After about 6 kilometers, the trail skirts a gravel bar on the river's edge and passes beneath sharp cliffs. This is the first designated camping area, with sites on the gravel bar and immediately following in the woods.

Tidbit The last time Vancouver Island was completely covered in ice was about 10,000 years ago. This period of glaciation had a major hand in shaping the mountainous landscape seen today.

Be sure to take advantage of the food cache if you are staying overnight.

Following the first campsite, the trail passes over a wooden bridge and a series of waterfalls. This is Butterwort Creek. For a rewarding side trip, follow an unmarked route up the far side of the falls for five to ten minutes to a pool where a 20-plus-meter cascade drops onto the rocks below. This is one of the nicest views on Butterwort Creek and is also a great photo opportunity.

After Butterwort Creek, the trail rises gradually and passes over a number of waterfalls rushing down to join the Elk River. Elk Falls is the last and largest cascade before the lake, and marks the spillway of the lake's overflow from a 1946 earthquake in which a chunk of Mount Colonel Foster slid down the hillside into the water. Surrounded by the brush of pioneering species such as scrub alder, salmonberry, and willow, the second campsite (9 kilometers) is on this spillway and lies about two hours from Landslide Lake. (Note that camping is not permitted at Landslide Lake.) During this last stretch, the trail winds from spillway gravel to forest, then across the Elk River via a footbridge. Once on bare rock, the remaining trail ascends gradually and is marked by rock cairns signaling the way to the top.

Although Landslide Lake is the official destination of this hike, it is also the entry point to Iceberg Lake, Mount Colonel Foster, and a number of unofficial routes beyond. To get to Iceberg Lake and the glacier, follow the east side of Landslide Lake via a route marked by flagging ribbons, and then climb the rocky waterfall to the glacier. This route is not maintained and takes approximately two hours one-way. If doing a multiday trip, this view provides a good luncheon stop on the second day.

Key points (km)

0.0 Start at the Elk River Trailhead, located off Highway 28. The trail begins as a gravel pathway heading away from the parking lot.

2.7 The trail crosses a creek and reaches an old camping area.

4.0 The trail crosses a creek.

4.8 The trail crosses another creek.

◀ *Butterwort Creek ambles through an enchanting forest on the Elk River Trail.*

prickly branchlets. Watch for evidence of elevation in the alpine wildflowers, which go from seed to bloom as you ascend.

Higher up, the trail opens onto a ridge affording the first unimpeded views of Buttle Lake and Auger Mountain. Cliffs marbled with white limestone line the path, which quickly vaults onto bare rock and up the ridge through further alpine wildflowers. This is just a sample of what lies over the ridge. Continue up and see chutes and meadows ablaze with mountain heather, lupine, aster, columbine, paintbrush, anemone, arnica, and more. The official park trail ends here, but further exploration along a well-trod route leads you northwest past a limestone and wildflower wonderland to Limestone, Globe Flower, and Marsh Marigold Lakes (in quick succession) and designated camping areas. Further routes also lead to Mount McBride, Morrison Spire, and Greig Ridge, all of which should only be attempted by experienced hikers with proper equipment. Wheaton Hut, beyond Globe Flower Lake, is available on a first-come, first-served basis.

Options: A challenging loop from Marble Meadows to Mount Philips across Philips Ridge takes you down on the opposite side of Phillips Creek. This is just one of many difficult ridge routes accessible from Marble Meadows Trail.

Hike Information

Trail Contact
B.C. Parks: Web site wlapwww.gov.bc.ca/bcparks.

Fees/Permits
An overnight backcountry camping fee of $5.00 per person, per night is required for overnight stays. There are twenty marine campsites located on Buttle Lake.

Local Information
Campbell River Visitor Info Center, P.O. Box 400, 1235 Shoppers Row, Campbell River, BC V9W 5B6; toll-free (800) 463–4386; phone (250) 287–4636; Web site www.campbellriver chamber.ca/vic.html; e-mail visitor info@campbellriverchamber.ca.

Maps/Brochures
NTS Map 92 F/12.
Strathcona Provincial Park brochure.

29

Upper Myra Falls

Suitable for the whole family, the hike to the upper cascades of the Myra River follows a relatively level path through mature forest. Highlights include the close-up view of Upper Myra Falls, and a forest punctuated by large examples of western hemlock and western red cedar that makes for a cool retreat on a hot day.

Distance: 3 kilometers.
Approximate hiking time: 1 hour.
Difficulty: Easy.
Type of hike: A well-marked forested trail.

Elevation gain: 50 meters.
Best season: June to September.
Land status: Provincial park.

Finding the trailhead: To reach Upper Myra Falls, follow Highway 28 from Campbell River to the eastern portal of Strathcona Park at the junction of Upper Campbell and Buttle Lakes. Turn left onto Western Mines Road and drive the length of Buttle Lake to where the road intersects the operations of the Westmin Mine. The trail starts behind the processing buildings, where the road ends at a gravel lot marked with signs. This is also the access to Tennant Lake and Phillips Ridge Trails. Follow the gated gravel road for approximately 700 meters, watching for a sign on your right marking access to Upper Myra Falls. (Do not be deterred by the DANGER, EXPLOSIVES signs—but by all means heed their advice and refrain from smoking.)

The hike: The majority of rocks in Strathcona Park are igneous—rocks formed by the solidification of molten matter. Some of these include basalt (black to dark gray with a granular appearance), rhyolite (white to gray, embracing the ore deposits in the Myra Falls mine), and granite (pink to dark gray with a coarse grain). If you can get by the mine and the danger signs without balking, you will see little further evidence of human activity in the park. This trail is a light hike for a morning or afternoon outing with the whole family that passes through mature western hemlock, western red cedar, and Douglas fir. Gradual switchbacks and straightaways lead you through fallen giants, rocky crags, and wild huckleberries. The trail ends at a boardwalk bridge overlooking Upper Myra Falls, a tall but narrow waterfall of stunning beauty. The overhead canopy provides natural coverage on a rainy day.

Douglas Fir

The Douglas fir is not really a fir at all, but a *pseudotsuga* or false hemlock. It gets its name from David Douglas, the Scottish botanist who introduced many of the province's evergreens to Europe. Look for the Douglas fir throughout Vancouver Island.

Upper Myra Falls

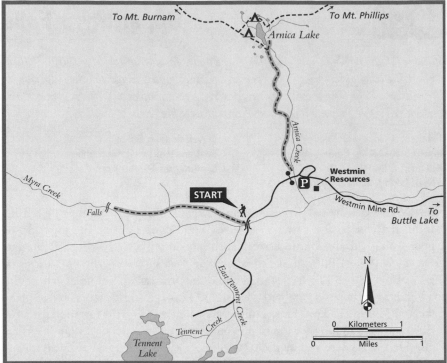

Hike Information

🕐 Trail Contact
B.C. Parks: Web site wlapwww.gov.bc.ca/bcparks.

💲 Fees/Permits
An overnight backcountry camping fee of $5.00 per person, per night is required for overnight stays.

❓ Local Information
Campbell River Visitor Info Center,
P. O. Box 400, 1235 Shoppers Row,
Campbell River, BC V9W 5B6; toll-free
(800) 463–4386; phone (250) 287–
4636; Web site www.campbellriver
chamber.ca/vic.html; e-mail visitor
info@campbellriverchamber.ca.

🅰 Maps/Brochures
NTS Map 92 F/12.
Strathcona Provincial Park brochure.

The sight and sounds of Upper Myra Falls offer ample rewards to hikers who make the trip.

30

Bedwell Lake

This vigorous hike through low- to middle-elevation forest leads to one of the more popular backcountry camping areas in the park. Pick up the trail at the south end of Buttle Lake and walk through mature forest and a fen wonderland to two craggy lakes. Both Bedwell and Baby Bedwell offer low-impact camping on tenting platforms. Food caches are available to outwit the bears. Bedwell Lake is the jumping-off point for a number of popular alpine routes, all of which take in the snowcapped peaks of Strathcona Park. Treat this as a destination hike or just one of the stops on a longer alpine adventure.

Distance: 6 kilometers.
Approximate hiking time: 3 hours.
Difficulty: Difficult.
Type of hike: A well-trod forest path of switchbacks, staircases, and footbridges. Be prepared for steep climbs on rocky, eroded paths.
Elevation gain: 600 meters.
Best season: August and September.
Land status: Provincial park.

Finding the trailhead: Follow Highway 28 from Campbell River to the eastern portal of Strathcona Park at the junction of Upper Campbell and Buttle Lakes. Turn left onto Western Mines Road and drive the length of Buttle Lake. Turn left again as you round the bottom of the lake onto Thelwood Valley–Jim Mitchell Lake Road and drive a further 6.8 kilometers over a rough gravel road that winds steeply upward. Park at the registration area and walk up the road to where a trailhead sign is hidden in the woods on your left. Backcountry fees are in effect for overnight visitors only.

The hike: The trail starts as an easy hike through middle-elevation mature forest. After a suspension bridge, the flat grade quickly gives way to steeper switchbacks, winding up the valley above Thelwood Creek and over its many tributaries. Watch for large examples of yellow cedar towering over the trail. After leaving Thelwood Creek, the trail moves sharply up the rocky landscape over more switchbacks and staircases to a fen area complete with marsh

Yellow Cedar

Yellow cedar, or *Chamaecyparis nootkatensis*, was first identified in Nootka Sound along the Island's west coast. During the last century, yellow cedar was highly prized by boatbuilders who recognized superior strength and quality in the tree's wood. Today yellow cedar is still used in boatbuilding and grows in deep, slightly acidic, moist soils and in alpine areas.

Bedwell Lake

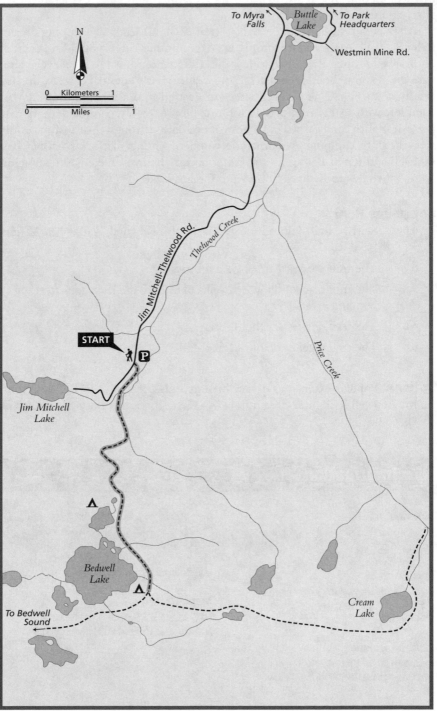

To Myra Falls

Buttle Lake

To Park Headquarters

Westmin Mine Rd.

N

0 Kilometers 1

0 Miles 1

Jim Mitchell-Thelwood Rd.

Thelwood Creek

Price Creek

START

P

Jim Mitchell Lake

Bedwell Lake

To Bedwell Sound

Cream Lake

marigold and standing water. A boardwalk protects the sensitive ground along this section of trail and provides for dry feet. Surrounding trees include mountain hemlock and amabilis fir.

After about an hour and a half, a trail offshoot leads to camping areas at Baby Bedwell. After 2 more kilometers over another ridge, you'll find camping on Bedwell proper. Be sure to follow the trail marker down to lake level—alternate routes and braided trails on the ridge viewpoint make trail direction briefly confusing. The Bedwell sites are nestled into a subalpine wonderland complete with a steel-reinforced outhouse (and, possibly, complementary reading material), a food cache, and a network of paths through the sensitive undergrowth. Both camping areas include wooden tenting platforms—six at Baby Bedwell and ten at Bedwell—and water access. Bedwell Lake is the launching point for routes to Bedwell Sound and Cream Lake.

Key points (km)

0.0 Start at the trailhead located just off Thelwood Valley–Jim Mitchell Lake Road.

0.7 The trail crosses a creek via a footbridge.

3.8 The trail reaches Baby Bedwell Lake. Take the right fork to reach the camping area.

4.6 The trail crosses another creek.

6.0 The trail reaches Bedwell Lake.

Options: Popular extensions of this hike include the routes to Bedwell Sound via the Bedwell River and Cream Lake via Little Jim Lake. Both of these routes are difficult.

Hike Information

☏ Trail Contact
B.C. Parks: Web site wlapwww.gov.bc.ca/bcparks.

$ Fees/Permits
An overnight backcountry camping fee of $5.00 per person, per night is required for overnight stays.

? Local Information
Campbell River Visitor Info Center, P. O. Box 400, 1235 Shoppers Row,

Campbell River, BC V9W 5B6; toll-free (800) 463–4386; phone (250) 287–4636; Web site www.campbellriverchamber.ca/vic.html; e-mail visitor info@campbellriverchamber.ca.

↡ Maps/Brochures
NTS Maps 92 F/5 and 92 F/12. **Strathcona Provincial Park** brochure.

Whether viewed on a foggy afternoon or a clear morning, Bedwell Lake possesses a serene beauty.

Mid-Island Honorable Mentions

Top Bridge Trail

This easy hike between Top Bridge and Industrial Way in Parksville is a well-traveled nature walk that traverses relatively flat terrain along the north end of the Englishman River. The trail begins at two access points, one located at the south end of Parksville just off Highway 19A on Industrial Way, and another off Highway 19 outside of town. For this second entrance, turn right off Highway 19 onto Kaye Road by the weigh scales south of Parksville. Take a second right onto Chattell Road and drive to where a gravel area provides ample parking. This is also a popular swimming spot. The regional district has plans to build a bridge across the river, linking this access to Allsbrook Road and eventually a corridor running all the way to Englishman River Falls. While sections of this trail pass through an old gravel pit and under Highway 19, there are some lovely sights where the trail skirts the Englishman River. Here the river meanders through emerald pools and past a craggy landscape filled with mature stands of Douglas fir and western red cedar. Painted rocks mark authorized passage through private property north of the railroad tracks. Currently the trail extends at the north end across Highway 19A and follows a road route to Rathtrevor Provincial Park. The total distance from Rathtrevor Beach to Top Bridge is 5 kilometers one-way. For more information, contact the Regional District of Nanaimo Recreation and Parks, P.O. Box 1119, Parksville, BC V9P 2H2; phone (250) 248–3252 or (877) 607–4111; Web site www.rdn.bc.ca.

Lacy Lake

After crossing a suspension bridge, the trail ascends a well-groomed path through Horne Lake Provincial Park in the direction of the caves that are marked on a map at the park entrance. About twenty minutes past the trailhead, the trail leaves the park and continues on an old, overgrown road. Following a path that was used by aboriginal peoples as a trading route, and by Captain Horne, this barely apparent trail starts at one of the turns in the park path. Due to the unmarked nature of this trail, it is best hiked with a compass. Turning left off the park trail, follow the old road south through a second-growth canopy. The trail ascends to a clearing near some power lines and a gate. Follow the power lines until you come to Lacy Lake. Note that logging roads crisscross this trail at several intervals. Horne Lake Provincial Park is located 60 kilometers north of Nanaimo off Highway 19 or 19A (Island Highway) near Qualicum Beach. Look for the park signs at the Horne Lake exit and follow the signs (more than 10 km) onto gravel logging roads until you come to the last parking lot. For more information about Horne Lake Provincial Park, contact B.C. Parks at wlapwww.gov.bc.ca/bcparks.

North
Island

When Captain James Cook made contact with the Island's aboriginal people at the west coast village of Yuquot in 1778, there were an estimated 25,000 people living on northern Vancouver Island. Since that time the northern portion of the Island has seen settlers from places as far away as Norway, Denmark, and Finland, many of whom came to work in the Island's rich industries of fishing, logging, and mining. While these industries still support most communities in the region, many are working to reconcile the needs of people, fish, and wildlife by moving toward alternative methods of resource extraction and by embracing new industries.

For hikers, the north Island is a place of vast wilderness. Okay, its claim to fame may still be the world's largest burl (twenty-two tons), but that hasn't stopped the region from becoming the home of some of the Island's finest hiking destinations, including Cape Scott Provincial Park. For geology buffs, the area also sports examples of some of the oldest rock formations on Vancouver Island, visible in the limestone formations located along the San Josef Wagon Road just outside Holberg. This limestone originated some 300 million years ago when an ancient sea still covered the area.

Like other portions of Vancouver Island, the northern region sees heavy accumulations of precipitation—nearly 1,766 millimeters annually—and annual temperatures averaging at around 8 degrees C. But because the region is also home to the most extensive populations of some of the Island's wildest inhabitants—whales, cougar, black bear, and seabirds—hiking on the north Island often involves getting up close and personal with wildlife. This is wilderness at its best: isolated beaches, towering rain forests, intriguing human history, and plenty of wilderness. Let's do our best to keep it that way.

31

Schoen Lake

Locate this rugged series of boat access hiking trails and routes via Schoen Lake Provincial Park near the Mount Cain Ski Area. The main trail from the Schoen Lake base camp explores the stunning Nisnak Valley, where multiple mountain peaks overlook a pristine lake. This trail also features large examples of mature western hemlock and red cedar. Paddle your canoe or kayak to the trailhead, where several routes offer day and overnight excursions. Alternate access via Adam River Main is also available for those without water transportation.

Distance: 6 kilometers from Schoen Lake to Adam River.

Approximate hiking time: 2 hours. For other routes in Schoen Lake Provincial Park, please see options below.

Difficulty: Difficult. Topographic maps are a necessity when traveling in the park. Be prepared for slippery log crossings and unexpected changes in weather.

Type of hike: A rough trail that quickly degenerates into a route marked only by flagging tape

and a progressively more obscure footpath. While the trail to Nisnak Lake can be accessed from both ends, the Schoen Lake route (accessible only by boat) is the easiest to navigate. None of the routes in this area is maintained, though most are flagged on a regular basis.

Elevation gain: 300 meters.

Best season: June to September. Snow may linger in the valley well into summer.

Land status: Provincial park.

Finding the trailhead: Traveling north on the Inland Island Highway (19) from Campbell River, turn left (east) onto the road marked MOUNT CAIN–SCHOEN LAKE, approximately 55 kilometers past Sayward. As you leave the highway, the road will fork. Take the left fork and follow it for approximately 2 kilometers. When the road forks again, turn right and follow the fork for another 3 kilometers. Here the road forks a third time. The left fork ascends Mount Cain to the ski area. Take the right fork (Davie Road) and drive for a bumpy 8 kilometers to Schoen Lake. Signs indicate the start of the park, as well as a day-use, boat-launch, and campground area. There is a fee for staying overnight in the campground. Park your car at the day-use area and launch from the beach. The trailhead is at the end of the lake, approximately 5 kilometers from the parking lot. Land your canoe or kayak in a grove of cedars at the foot of Mount Schoen and follow trail markers east from the campsite.

The hike: The trail starts just south of the campsite at the northeast end of Schoen Lake. Follow the flagging through massive cedars in a southeasterly direction to a bench above the lake. Here the trail levels out and passes through spectacular old-growth forest dominated by hemlock and huckleberry.

Schoen Lake

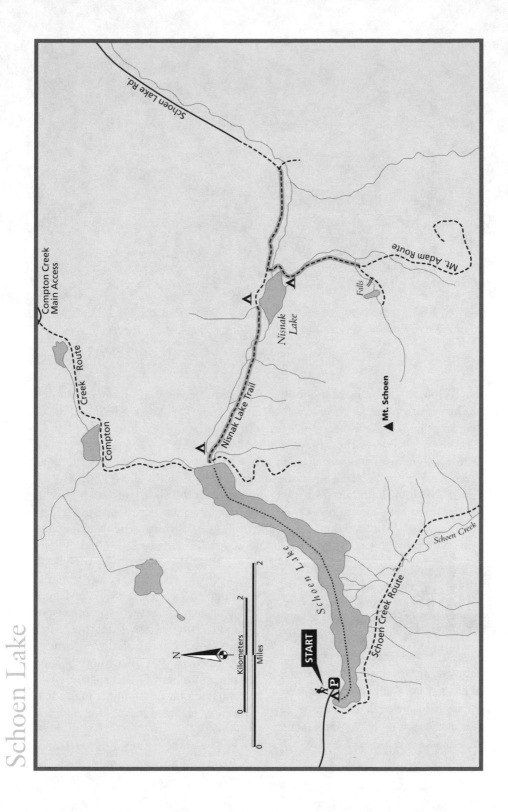

The hike to Nisnak Lake starts with a 5-kilometer paddle down the length of Schoen Lake.

While old blazes mark the trail, most have healed over, resulting in a swatch of black bark at eye level. Watch for flagging and a small, meandering footpath cutting through the moss, or rely on your topographic map.

The trail follows the valley south of Nisnak Creek, passing through two slides before crossing over a fallen log. The second, larger slide is the most recent and has obliterated any trace of flagging through the slide's path. To pick up the trail on the other side, travel uphill across the slide and watch for ribbons. From here the trail descends to Nisnak Creek and crosses at the largest bend in the river (noted on topographic maps as an obvious switchback). By the time you reach this crossing, you should be heading due east.

> **Tidbit**
>
> Schoen Lake Provincial Park is an 8,430-hectare wilderness park protecting old-growth forests, glaciers, waterways, and meadows, as well as elk and fish habitat. While the trails in the park are barely maintained, the area offers challenging routes for the experienced hiker who is fully self-sufficient.

From the north side of Nisnak Creek, the trail moves away from the water and parallels the lake before emerging at a small camping spot about 600 meters from the creek crossing. Nisnak Lake affords a spectacular view of Mount Schoen and a number of other distant peaks unnamed on topographic maps. It is also a secluded haven for summer loons.

For those continuing to Upper Adam Main, head east through the meadows until you reach the Adam River. From this crossing the road is a further 400 meters southeast. An alternate route from Nisnak Lake follows a creek valley south to Schoen Falls and to the top of a secondary peak. This hike offers more valley views and a look at Mount Nora.

Key points (km)

0.0 Start at the trailhead located in the cedar grove campsite at the northeastern end of Schoen Lake.

0.2 The trail crosses a creek.

1.2 The trail crosses a second creek.

1.7 The trail passes through a small slide area.

1.9 The trail crosses a third creek.

2.0 The trail passes through a large alder slide.

2.2 The trail crosses Nisnak Creek.

3.0 The trail reaches a campsite on Nisnak Lake.

4.0 The trail reaches the meadows.

5.7 The trail reaches the Adam River.

6.2 The trail reaches Upper Adam Main.

Options: There are a number of alternate routes in Schoen Lake Provincial Park. Some of these include the Schoen Creek Route (4.3 km), which follows Schoen Creek from the south side of Schoen Lake; the Compton Creek Route (5.3 km), which follows Compton Creek to the Adam River; Schoen Falls and a secondary peak of Mount Schoen (9 km), which heads south from Nisnak Lake and follows an unnamed creek up the peak to the east of Mount Schoen; and Schoen Mountain (2.5 km), which climbs the west side of Mount Schoen from the wilderness campsite on Schoen Lake.

Hike Information

◑ Trail Contact
B.C. Parks: Web site wlapwww.gov.bc. ca/bcparks.

⑤ Fees/Permits
No fees or permits required. To stay overnight in the Schoen Lake Provincial Park campground, there is a fee of $9.00 per party.

❓ Local Information
Sayward Chamber of Commerce, P. O. Box 70, Sayward, BC V0P 1R0; phone/fax (250) 282–3845; Web site www.sayward.com; e-mail info@sayward.com.

◐ Maps/Brochures
NTS Map 92 L/1.

Raft Cove

Located within a small coastal park, this short hike through a rugged forest of western hemlock, western red cedar, and Sitka spruce leads to the wide-open beaches of Raft Cove. For further exploring, walk the beach route along an ever-changing shoreline to view sea stacks and tidal pools. (Beach portions are best hiked at low tide.) Raft Cove is also a popular surfing destination for north Islanders.

Distance: Up to 6 kilometers.
Approximate hiking time: Up to 3 hours of forest and beach walking.
Difficulty: The forest trail is difficult due to steep stairs, gnarled roots, and a general lack of maintenance. The beach trail is moderate due to rock scramble and shifting tides.

Type of hike: A rough trail through muddy terrain. This trail also includes many slippery log crossings.
Elevation gain: No significant elevation gains.
Best season: Year-round, though winter storms make for wet camping.
Land status: Provincial park.

Finding the trailhead: Access to Raft Cove Provincial Park is via a combination of paved highways and gravel logging roads. From Port McNeill, travel north along Highway 19 to the Port Hardy turnoff. Port Hardy is the northern terminus of Highway 19 and offers a final stop for guaranteed supplies of food, gas, and tourist information. (While the town of Holberg does have a gas, station and restaurant, supplies are not always readily available.) Check in at the tourist information center for up-to-date visitor brochures and an indispensable map of north Island logging roads.

Continuing west at the turnoff, follow posted signs to Cape Scott. The first 20 kilometers of this gravel road are public and maintained on a regular basis. Shortly before Holberg, the road switches to private ownership and conditions are considerably more challenging. Hikers traveling in this area are advised to take along two spare tires.

Approximately 10 kilometers outside Holberg, turn left onto Ronning Main. Follow Ronning Main for 11 kilometers, and then turn left onto Ronning 700. The road terminates after a kilometer at the Raft Cove Trailhead.

The hike: The trail begins with a series of steep stairs descending to the forest floor. Bridges and log crossings with thin bits of gripping rope are the norm on this trail. Be prepared to navigate root-infested mud holes and large, slippery nurse logs. Fancy footwork should be expected in this portion of the Quatsino rain forest. Misleading flagging may cause confusion halfway along the trail. Stick to the main path and listen for the sound of the surf pounding onto the beach. The final leg of this hike moves through a dense thicket of salal, tunneled no doubt by short individuals. The stoop is short-lived, howev-

Raft Cove

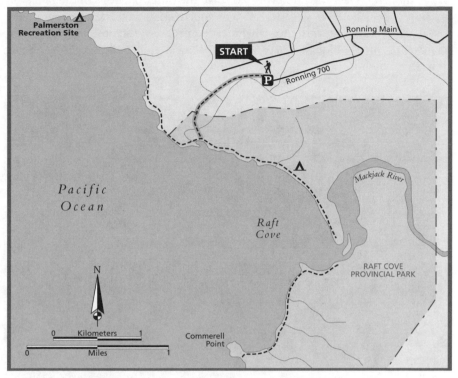

er, and you soon emerge onto a vast beach.

Once onto the beach, exploration in several directions is possible. Traveling south to the Mackjack River, you will find approximately 2 kilometers of rocky shoreline and firm sand. The Mackjack River presents a difficult crossing for those who dislike wet feet (or thighs). Waiting until low tide only partially solves this problem. Cross at the lowest tide and be prepared to get wet. Beyond the river is a further section of park containing an old cabin once belonging to Cape Scott pioneer Willie Hecht, who settled in the area in 1913. The best freshwater supply is found in the stream emptying near this cabin, on the south side of the river. The easy walking continues on the other side of the stream and ends with a short-cut across Commerell Point.

Traveling north from the forest trail, the route extends to a second access off the end of Coast Main. This section of the hike offers cobble and rocky shorelines, as well as a walk-in forest recreation camp-

Because Raft Cove Provincial Park faces out to the open Pacific, the beaches are often buffeted by high winds and deluged with rain. Be sure to bring ample rain gear and plenty of warm layers year-round.

ground with five sites. Camping is permitted throughout Raft Cove Provincial Park, though no facilities are provided. Like the other portions of the hike, this section is best done at low tide. While approximately 1.3 kilometers of the beach at Raft Cove is sand, the remainder requires some scrambling over rocks, driftwood, and boulders. Carry a copy of local tide tables to avoid being trapped at high tide.

The hike to Raft Cove involves many slippery log crossings. Some, unlike this one near the start of the trail, do not afford the luxury of gripping ropes.

Salal

Salal is a common Island plant that grows from 0.2 to 5 meters tall, forming dense barriers on the windswept beaches off the Island's west coast. Its oval leaves have a shiny, leathery appearance and are used in flower arrangements all over the world. Although somewhat hairy, its berries have a high pectin content and are excellent additions to jams and jellies. They were once a major food source for the Island's first peoples.

Key points (km)

0.0   Start hiking from the Raft Cove Trailhead. The trail veers immediately down a series of steep steps.

0.7   The trail rises to a slightly higher plateau where there is less mud.

0.9   The trail reaches Raft Cove beach. Turn left to reach the Mackjack River and Willie Hecht's cabin. Turn right for cobble beaches and Palmerston Recreation Site.

2.0   (Left from forest trail) The trail reaches the Mackjack River. Cross the river at its mouth during the lowest tide.

2.2   The trail reaches Willie Hecht's cabin. This cabin apparently sleeps four, and is used on a first-come, first-served basis.

3.2   The trail reaches Commerell Point, where a short extension veers inland across the small peninsula.

4.0   (Right from forest trail) The trail reaches Palmerston Recreation Site. This is a forest recreation site, which can be accessed via Coast Main. Be warned that this is a route rather than a trail.

Hike Information

🕻 Trail Contact
B.C. Parks: Web site wlapwww.gov.bc.ca/bcparks.

$ Fees/Permits
No fees or permits required.

❓ Local Information
Port Hardy Chamber of Commerce, 7250 Market Street, Port Hardy, BC

VON 2P0; phone (250) 949–7622; fax (250) 949–6653; Web site www.ph-chamber.bc.ca; e-mail phcc@island.net.

 Maps/Brochures
NTS Map 102 I/9.
Northern Vancouver Island Region Visitors Guide Map (Western Forest Products).

33 San Josef Bay/Mount St. Patrick

This dramatic hike begins by following a level trail to San Josef Bay on the northwest coast of Vancouver Island. Where the San Josef River enters the sea, vast sand beaches complete with caves and sea stacks await the shoreline explorer. For those interested in a spectacular viewpoint, a rugged trail leads from the beach to the peak of Mount St. Patrick, offering a 360-degree panorama of the Cape Scott coastline, the Scott Islands, and the open Pacific.

Distance: 8 kilometers.
Approximate hiking time: 3½ hours.
Difficulty: From the parking lot to San Josef Bay, the trail is easy. After leaving the second beach and beginning the ascent of Mount St. Patrick, the trail becomes difficult.

Type of hike: An easy walk via a forested footpath to the surf-tossed shores of San Josef Bay followed by a more challenging ascent up Mount St. Patrick over deadfall, slippery logs, and root mazes.
Elevation gain: 442 meters.
Best season: May to September.
Land status: Provincial park.

Finding the trailhead: Access to Cape Scott Provincial Park is via a combination of paved highways and gravel logging roads. From Port McNeill, travel north along Highway 19 to the Port Hardy turnoff. Port Hardy is the northern terminus of Highway 19 and offers a final stop for guaranteed supplies of food, gas, and tourist information. (While the town of Holberg does have a gas station and restaurant, supplies are not always readily available.) Check in at the tourist information center for up-to-date visitor brochures and an indispensable map of north Island logging roads.

Continuing west at the turnoff, follow posted signs to Cape Scott. The first 20 kilometers of this gravel road are public and maintained on a regular basis. Shortly before Holberg, the road switches to private ownership and conditions are considerably more challenging. Hikers traveling to Cape Scott are advised to take along two spare tires.

Tidbit Less than 2 kilometers outside Holberg, the San Josef Wagon Road begins just north of San Josef Main. Forged by hearty settlers as a link between Holberg and Cape Scott, the road stretches for nearly 20 kilometers.

Three kilometers outside Holberg, turn right (west) onto San Josef Main and follow signs to the park. The parking lot and trailhead are located 2 kilometers beyond the San Josef Recreation Site. This site offers eleven campsites and a modest boat launch for kayaks and canoes. The total logging road travel for this hike is 65 kilometers.

San Josef Bay/Mount St. Patrick

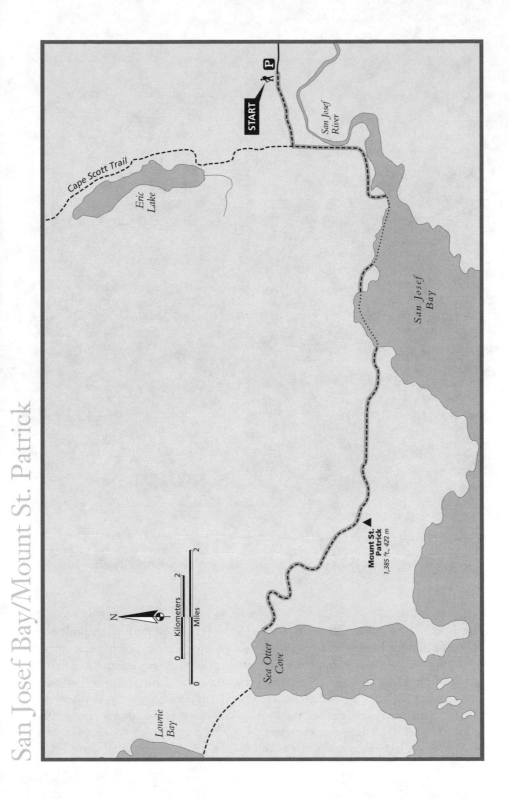

Curious-looking sea stacks—like these in San Josef Bay—are formed by dramatic wave action pummeling the shoreline.

The hike: The San Josef Bay area of Cape Scott Provincial Park offers limitless opportunities for hikers, bird-watchers, tidal pool explorers, and history buffs. Beginning at the main parking lot and passing through swampland and old-growth forests, the trail provides glimpses of the second European settlement attempted at the cape. Thanks to interpretive displays and measures to preserve the park's history, hikers can see the remains of settlements built between 1908 and 1917. Before setting out on the trail, pick up a copy of the Cape Scott brochure, available through north Island tourist information centers and B.C.

Parks. The brochure details the locations of more than twenty-five points of interest related to the settlers and their surrounding wilderness.

For hikers interested in an overnight stay, San Josef Bay offers numerous campsites beyond the high-tide area. Food caches and outhouses are available at both beaches. The trail to the first beach follows a wide gravel walkway from the parking lot.

Bald eagles generally make their nests in the tops of tall snags. The Triangle Islands, visible from the top of Mount St. Patrick in the Scott Island archipelago, are one of the few places these eagles have been known to nest on the ground.

Hiking the trail to Mount St. Patrick is considerably easier at tides below 2 meters, when flat expanses of sand beach are exposed and accessible. If you find yourself trapped by high tides and in need of an overland route, locate a rough trail at the northern end of the first beach where a rope leads up a rocky path. Depending on the level of the tides, you may be able to descend to the second beach by the midtide trail, or by an alternate route farther along. Continue west to the end of the second beach where the trail into the woods is marked by a suspended float. The trail ascends sharply up the mountain, over exposed roots and fallen logs to the peaks of Mount St. Patrick.

From Mount St. Patrick, the view is 360 degrees. On a clear day the Scott Islands, considered to be the most important seabird area in Pacific Canada, are visible in the distance. They are home to more than 70 percent of the world's population of the Cassin's auklet and provide breeding, nesting, and foraging habitat for other migratory seabirds. Under their current designation as an ecological reserve, the Scott Islands are not protected from activities that harm foraging habitat. A number of nonprofit groups are actively working with First Nations, governments, and other groups to include the Scott Islands in a network of marine protected areas.

Key points (km)

0.0   Start at the Cape Scott Provincial Park Trailhead, located at the end of San Josef Main.

0.9   The trail reaches a junction. Turn left for San Josef Bay.

1.0   The trail passes through a swamp over a boardwalk.

1.7   The trail passes an interpretive display and side trail on the left to the San Josef River.

2.5   The trail reaches First Beach, on the San Josef River estuary. Turn right.

3.7   The trail reaches Second Beach and rock formations known as sea stacks.

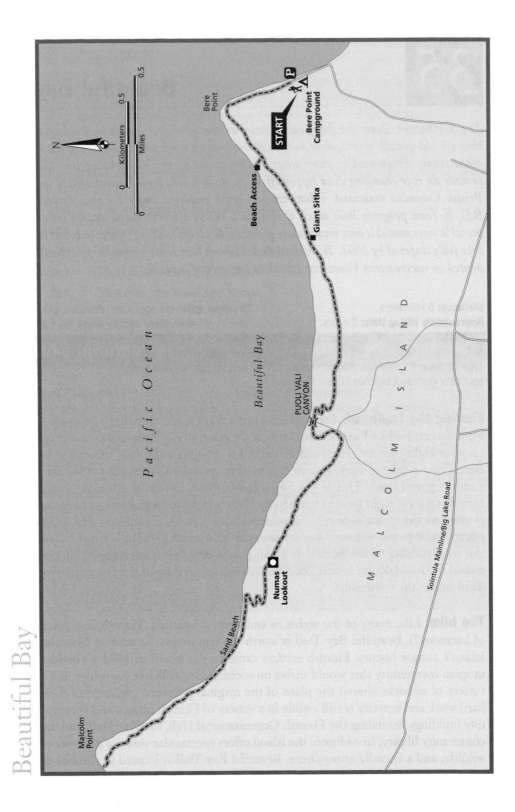

Pacific Ocean

Malcolm
Point

Sand Beach

Numas
Lookout

PUOLI VALI
CANYON

Beautiful Bay

Beach Access

Giant Sitka

Bere
Point

START

Bere Point
Campground

P

MALCOLM ISLAND

Sointula Mainline/Big Lake Road

N

Kilometers
0   0.5

Miles
0   0.5

the Bere Point Campground and provides access to several kilometers of pebble and cobble beaches. Camping in the designated campground is available on a first-come, first-served basis, and campers are asked to bring their own water.

Tidbit *Puoli Vali* means "halfway along the journey" in Finnish. The canyon is also known for gold panning, which took place on the beach in the 1930s.

Beyond the campground, the trail rounds Bere Point and moves in and out of old-growth forests. From the beginning of the hike, evidence of the coast's dramatic weather can be seen on either side of the trail. On December 13, 2001, an unprecedented storm blew across Malcolm Island, knocking down trees along the island's northern coast. Pultney Point Lighthouse, at the western tip of the island, recorded winds of up to 112 knots (that's up to 207 km), the likes of which Malcolm Island had not seen in one hundred years. In the summer of 2002, island residents and Katimivik participants cleared the trail to the crossing at Puoli Vali Canyon. Plans are under way to repair the extensive damage to the trail's remaining 2.5 kilometers by 2003. Until that time, hikers can access Malcolm Point via the beach at low tide. While this is a difficult walk requiring fancy footwork (much of the beach is covered in uneven cobble), the view from the point offers further perspectives of the bay, Numas Islands, and beyond.

Key points (km)

0.0 Start at the trailhead located just beyond Bere Point Regional Campground.

0.2 Evidence of a major windstorm litters areas near the trail for the next several hundred meters.

0.7 First beach access.

1.0 The trail reaches a lookout.

1.3 The trail passes a giant Sitka spruce, approximately 65 meters tall.

2.5 The trail descends the stairs of Puoli Vali Canyon. Beach access is possible at this point.

2.7 The trail ascends stairs on the other side of Puoli Vali Canyon.

3.5 The trail reaches Numas Lookout.

3.9 The trail reaches another set of stairs.

4.2 The trail reaches a small sand beach.

5.1 The trail rounds Malcolm Point.

Options: Mateoja Heritage Trail offers further explorations into Sointula's human and natural history. This historic trail follows the path of Finnish pioneers John and Annamaria Mateoja along a hundred-year-old skid trail that extends to their former farm site a short distance from town. Other highlights farther along this 3.2-kilometer trail include Melvin's Bog, Duck Pond, and Big Lake. Start at the trailhead located just off Third Street behind the water tower.

Hike Information

Trail Contacts/Local Information
Port McNeill Chamber of Commerce, P. O. Box 129, Port McNeill, BC VON 2R0; phone (250) 956–3131; Web site www.portmcneill.net or www.island.net/~sointula; e-mail pmcc@island.net.

Fees/Permits
No fees or permits required.

Maps/Brochures
Beautiful Bay/Mateoja Heritage Trail Map brochure.

North Island Honorable Mentions

San Josef Wagon Road

The San Josef Wagon Road is located just outside the town of Holberg. Follow the signs for Cape Scott Provincial Park west from town, and turn right (north) where a small pull-in for cars and prominent signage indicates the start of the trailhead. This is the original route Danish settlers used to carry supplies between their settlement at the cape and Holberg. Though the road stretches for a level 18 kilometers, it is overgrown in places and only portions are used on a regular basis. Some highlights include limestone caves, a series of interpretive signs mounted at intervals along the eastern access, ancient car wrecks, a small cemetery, and the Ronning Garden. In 1910 Bernt Ronning purchased two hectares of land on the San Josef Wagon Road and spent the next fifty years cultivating plants and seedlings from all over the world. Two monkey puzzle trees now stand near the site of his former homestead. Daffodils, rhododendrons, flowering peaches, azaleas, Oriental maples, and even a small grove of eucalyptus surround them. The garden is located approximately 15 kilometers from Holberg and is currently maintained. For easier access to this

These Sitka spruce, located at Beautiful Bay on Malcolm Island, have withstood some of the Pacific Coast's most dramatic weather. ▶

The west coast o
Ucluelet, Bamfield, a
region's hiking trails
sand beaches, not t
national park. While
any region, it also re
"rogue" waves frequ
When the storms lif
reach through the cl
ers of a living bioma

Anthropologists e
along Vancouver Isla
logging arose and re
governments of Can
Council (NTC) Cen

Wind-stunted co
National Park, one
favorite Long Beach
and Tofino. Nestled
stretches for 10 kilo
Point, the official pa

To the south, th
stretches 70 kilomet
more rigorous exper
staircases should try
trail requires advanc

Trails in both sec
to woodlands. Black
mals inhabit wooded
seals, porpoises, and

For West Coast
within Vancouver).
is at (250) 726–4212
stration Office, Pac
V0R 3A0; phone
pacrim/; e-mail pacri

portion of the wa
Crossing Boardwa
turnoff on your rig
Commerce, 7250
949–7622; Web si

Ripple Rock

For years Seymou
land was one of t
America. Describe
vilest stretches of
peaks of danger lu
Ripple Rock sank
destroyed on Apri
Ripple Rock to a r
sponsored by the
this bit of naviga
mature forest to v
now infamous Rip
out point and the
River and turn rig
interpretive displa
moderate trail wit
a half one-way.

Mount Cain

Mount Cain is lo
Sayward, travel 5
signs mark access
the left, approxim
cial trails on Mou
hiked during the
the wildflowers a
difficult terrain, a
attempt to follow
Visitor Info Cent
V0N 2R0; phone
contact is the Mo

Juan de Fuca Marine Trail

Visit 47 kilometers of rugged coastal hiking along southern Vancouver Island's west coast. Depending on the time and length of your hike, you may see pristine waterfalls, nesting bald eagles, breaching orcas, pounding surf, and frolicking seals. Whenever you hike, you are guaranteed a rainbow of marine life and scenic coastal as well as forested landscapes. The B.C. government commissioned Juan de Fuca Trail in 1994 to commemorate the Commonwealth Games. While sections of the trail are gaining popularity (particularly China Beach to Mystic Beach, and sections near Botanical Beach), it is still possible to feel like the last person on earth in many places. Because of its proximity to Victoria and the relative brevity of its trail, Mystic Beach may look like tent city on a weekend.

Distance and approximate hiking time: Hiking the entire trail requires 3 to 5 days. Shorter segments are also possible using any of four trailheads. Some of the distances are: Juan de Fuca East Trailhead to Sombrio Beach, 29 kilometers; Sombrio Beach to Parkinson Creek, 8 kilometers; Parkinson Creek to Botanical Beach, 10 kilometers.

Difficulty: Juan de Fuca East Trailhead to Bear Beach campsite, moderate; Bear Beach to Sombrio Point, difficult; Sombrio Point to Botanical Beach, moderate; Botanical Beach to Botany Bay, easy.

Type of hike: Most of this trail is designed for challenging day or overnight hiking.

Elevation gain: Up and down over hilly terrain to a maximum of 160 meters.

Best season: This trail is open year-round, although the months of July to September offer the best chances of staying dry. Keep in mind that the Island's lowest daytime tides occur in summer. Stick to the warm season and you increase your chances to view the infamous biodiversity of west coast tidal pools. A pocket-size identification guide is a good addition to this trip and well worth the weight. Be sure to carry rain gear and appropriate footwear. Thanks to heavy rains, this trail has the potential to turn into a mudslide at any time of year.

Land status: Provincial park.

Finding the trailhead: Juan de Fuca Provincial Park extends from China Beach in the east, just west of the small town of Jordan River, to Botanical Beach in the west, near Port Renfrew. Four trailheads make it possible to hike the trail in smaller sections or all in one trip. Most hikers access the trail via Highway 14. Heading west from Victoria, follow the highway through the towns of Colwood and Sooke. The Juan de Fuca East Trailhead is 35 kilometers west of Sooke and is marked by provincial park signposts, next to the China Beach parking lot. The Sombrio Beach, Parkinson Creek, and Botanical Beach Trailheads follow in succession.

Transit providers also offer pickup and drop-off services along Juan de Fuca Trail. The West Coast Trail Express services all trailheads and will return you to your car if you drive to the trail yourself. See the end of this hike description for contact information. This is a good alternative for those seeking to avoid backtracking. However, vehicles left at trailheads may often be the targets of "smash and grabs." Be sure to secure your vehicle and leave no valuables inside.

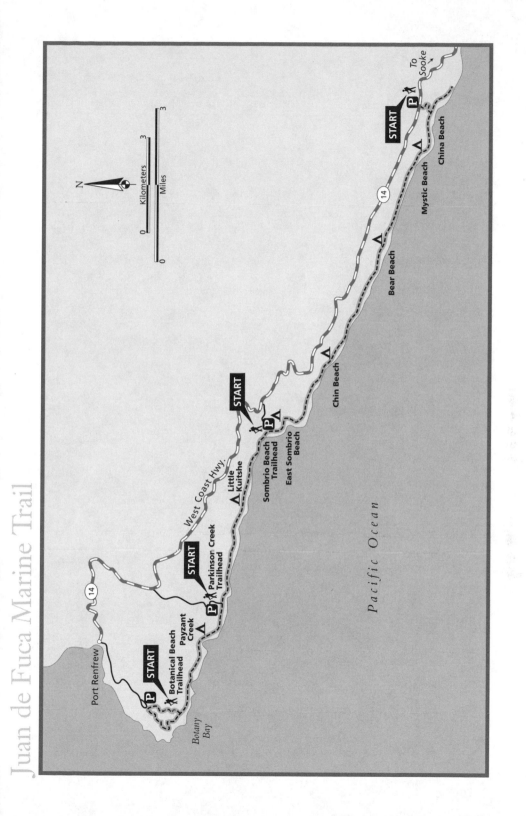

Juan de Fuca Marine Trail

The hike(s): The trail is marked by a well-used path and regular signage indicating distances to campsites. Certain legs of the trail follow the beach and may be cut off during high tides. Watch for orange floats hanging in shoreline trees. These mark access points where the trail winds back into the forest. Tide tables are available at local bookstores and marine supply stores and are posted at all trailheads and beach accesses. When daylight saving time is in effect, add one hour to tidal listings.

Designated walk-in campsites are available at Mystic Beach, Bear Beach, Chin Beach, East Sombrio, Little Kuitshe, and Payzant Creek. There are also wooden camping platforms at West Sombrio. When staying at these sites, hang all food out of reach of bears and use outhouse facilities where provided. Fresh water is available from a number of creeks along the trail. Filtering or boiling all drinking water is recommended.

Juan de Fuca East Trailhead to Sombrio Beach: One of our favorite sections, the Juan de Fuca East to Sombrio leg of the trail offers some of the best scenery with a variety of terrain. Park at the Juan de Fuca East Trailhead and you will pass through a dark forest of sweet-smelling conifers, then over a number of freshwater creeks winding their way to the sea. Two kilometers from the trailhead, a fallen giant fashioned into a wooden staircase marks the descent down to sandy Mystic Beach. This portion of the trail is usually busy, and tenting at the Mystic Beach campsite requires a willingness to get close to your neighbor.

Between Mystic and Bear Beaches, the trail gains elevation, providing a number of stunning lookout points to the ocean below. While this section of the trail may feel like your morning StairMaster workout, it is rated moderate and is a primer for what is to come. Bear Beach marks the second campsite, 9 kilometers from the Juan de Fuca East Trailhead. Here a rocky beach replaces the fine sand.

After the Bear Beach campsite, the trail graduates from moderate to difficult as you navigate grueling switchbacks, skirt Magdalena Point, and head for rocky Chin Beach. If you are looking to test your mettle, this portion of the trail is for you. Drink plenty of water and watch your footwork over exposed roots and muddy sections. When you arrive at the Chin Beach campsite, 21 kilometers in, you will find the hiker population considerably thinner.

Leaving Chin Beach, the difficulty eases slightly as the trail leaves behind the sound of the crashing surf and heads back into the trees. After much meandering through a dark and silent forest, the trees open revealing daylight, salal, and (in season) hordes of wild berries. Moving along vast cliffs and rocky headlands, the trail emerges at Sombrio Point, approximately 29 kilometers from the Juan de Fuca East Trailhead. Here a crystal stream crashes down a brilliant waterfall onto the sandy beach below.

◀ *Take the time to stop and explore the shoreline along the Juan de Fuca Marine Trail. This waterfall, located near the Sombrio Beach trailhead, offers a speedy way to cool off.*

From Lake Cowichan, follow South Shore Road past Gordon Bay Provincial Park to Nitinat Main. Continue along Nitinat Main until you reach the junction with South Main. Turn left at South Main and continue to the Caycuse River Bridge. Follow directions as above from this point forward.

From Port Renfrew, follow the Lake Cowichan Connector north to Honeymoon Bay. Turn left onto South Shore Road (the road will become Nitinat Main) and follow this route until you reach the junction with South Main. Turn left onto South Main and continue to the Caycuse River Bridge. Follow directions as above from this point forward.

The hike: Volunteers from the Western Canada Wilderness Committee (WCWC) built the original trail into the Carmanah Valley as part of an effort to save the legendary trees here. At the time MacMillan Bloedel owned the license to log the area and took the WCWC to court to prevent them from trespassing on the land. WCWC won the right to continue building, however, and set up a research station in the canopy of the trees. Researchers later uncovered more than twenty new varieties of insects. WCWC has since built trails into a number of threatened wild areas, including Clayoquot Sound and the Walbran Valley.

Trails in the park lead either up or down Carmanah Creek. Before setting out, keep in mind that many sections of the trail are typically very muddy, especially during rainy winter months. Bring appropriate rain gear, warm clothing, and hiking boots. Campsites are located in four areas of the park: one at the trailhead, approximately 250 meters from the parking lot; another on a sandbar near the Three Sisters; a third at Grunt's Grove off Upper Valley Trail; and a fourth past Paradise Pool, where you'll find sandy spots to pitch a tent. Pit toilets are available at the trailhead, Grunt's Grove, and the Three Sisters campsites. A bear food cache is located at the Three Sisters campsite. Fires are not allowed at any of the sandbar locations. Water can be obtained close to the main parking lot and past the entrance to Valley Mist Trail, and can be filtered from Carmanah Creek. The park has no gas, food, telephone, or medical services.

From the parking lot, take the service road to the Valley Mist Trail. A ten-

A Brief History

In 1988 conservationist Randy Stoltmann and a friend came upon Carmanah Valley while hiking in the area. Both were inspired by the sight of the "legendary giants," and brought international attention to the rarity of the ancient trees, which were then scheduled for logging. In 1990 Randy's dedication resulted in the founding of Carmanah Pacific Provincial Park. Five years later B.C. Parks added the Lower Walbran Valley to what is now called Carmanah Walbran Provincial Park. The Randy Stoltmann Commemorative Grove, located just downstream of the Fallen Giant, remembers the conservationist, who died in 1994.

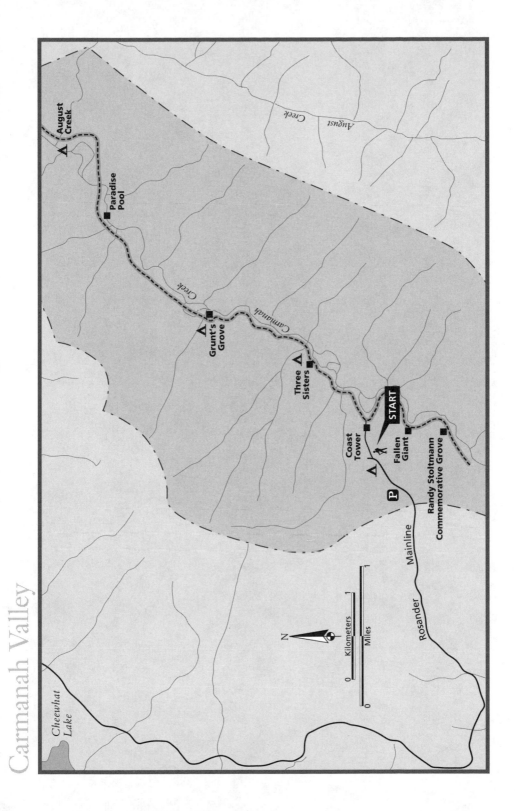

Carmanah Valley

minute downhill walk will lead you to the boardwalk. Note that this boardwalk is very slippery when wet. When you reach a sign at the junction telling you that Three Sisters Trail is to the left (forty minutes) and Heaven Grove Trail to the right (thirty-five minutes), continue on Upper Valley Trail by following the Three Sisters Trail indicator. On your way to the Three Sisters—a trio of Sitka spruce—you'll pass a hollow tree. When marveling at the park's green giants, obey the signs to stay on paths and behind ropes. This is so that plant-growth can recarpet the forest floor.

After viewing Three Sisters, the trail hugs the river for a stretch. Veering off the boardwalk, flagging tape appears at various points along the creek and at trail entrances. Follow the flagging across a minor creek to the other side. Once again, follow flagging on the other side of the creek until you come to Grunt's Grove. This spot offers camping by the water on sandy shores by large Sitka spruce. Leave Grunt's Grove and remain on the trail past the toilets until you arrive at Paradise Pool. Deep clear water surrounded by mossy banks is perfect for a hot-day dip or for enjoying a snack. At the time of publication, the path above Paradise Pool was not being maintained.

Key points (km)

0.0   Start at the trailhead by the Carmanah Walbran Provincial Park Headquarters.

1.2   The trail reaches Coast Tower.

1.5   The trail reaches the main junction and the end of the gravel path.

Upstream from the junction:

2.5   The trail reaches the Three Sisters and the first wilderness campsite. Good photo opportunities are available on the Sisters' viewing platform.

4.0   The trail reaches Grunt's Grove and the second wilderness campsite.

4.2   The trail crosses a secondary arm of Carmanah Creek twice in quick succession.

5.5   The trail reaches Paradise Pool. Enjoy good views of the creek's aqua-marine water.

5.7   The trail crosses Carmanah Creek.

7.5   The trail reaches August Creek and a third wilderness campsite.

Downstream from the junction:

2.0   The trail reaches Heaven Tree.

2.3   The trail reaches Fallen Giant.

2.6   The trail reaches Randy Stoltmann Commemorative Grove.

3.7   The trail closes beyond this point. Access to West Coast Trail is not permitted.

◀ *Take time to experience the ancient splendor of Three Sisters, a trio of Sitka spruce in the Carmanah Valley.*

Hike Information

Trail Contacts

B.C. Parks: Web site wlapwww.gov.bc.ca/bcparks.

TimberWest Forest Information Office, 125C South Shore Road, Lake Cowichan, BC V0R 2G0; phone (250) 749-3244; fax (250) 749-0187.

Ministry of Forests, South Island Forest District, 4885 Cherry Creek Road, Port Alberni, BC V9Y 8E9; phone (250) 731-3000; fax (250) 731-3010.

Fees/Permits

There is a backcountry camping fee of $5.00 per person, per night. No other fees or permits are required.

Local Information

Cowichan Tourism Association, 25 Canada Avenue, Duncan, BC V9L 1T3; phone (250) 715-0709; fax (250) 715-0710; Web site www.cowichan.bc.ca; e-mail tourism@cowichan.bc.ca.

Alberni Valley Visitor Info Center, Site 215, C-10, R.R. 2, Port Alberni, BC V9Y 7L6; phone (250) 724-6535; fax (250) 724-6560; Web site www.avcoc.com; e-mail avcoc@cedar.alberni.net.

Maps/Brochures

NTS Maps 92 C/10, 92 C/15.
Carmanah Walbran Provincial Park brochure.
South and Central Vancouver Island Recreation Map (Carmanah Forestry Society).
Recreation and Logging Road Guide (Weyerhauser).

Walbran Valley

Several options are available in this lush rain forest, home to some of the largest trees on Vancouver Island. Stroll on a recently completed loop just a short distance from the parking lot to take in a western red cedar measuring almost 5 meters in diameter, or hike one of the more strenuous routes along the valley's bottom for a multiday rain forest experience. Either way, be prepared for rough roads and unpredictable weather conditions, and be sure to bring your rain gear.

Distance: More than 30 kilometers of trail.
Approximate hiking times: Main Camp to Big Log Junction—1 to 2 hours; Big Log Junction to Anderson Lake—1 to 2 hours; Big Log Junction to Botley Lake—3 to 5 hours.
Difficulty: Moderate to difficult.
Type of hike: Volunteer-built trails and boardwalks with minimal signage.

Elevation gain: Varies with selected hike.
Best season: Trails are accessible year-round, but summer and fall hikes offer the best chances of staying dry. This is a bona fide rain forest, and appropriate rain gear is a must.
Land status: Provincial park and Tree Farm License 46 (TimberWest).

Walbran Valley

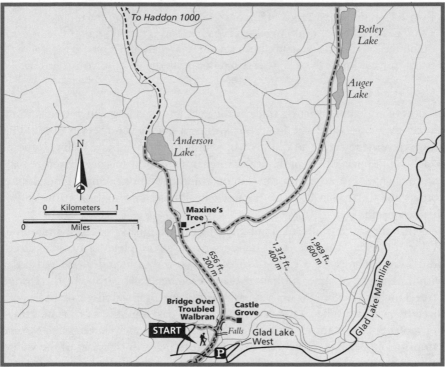

Finding the trailhead: Accessing the Walbran Valley without an accurate road map is at your own peril. In the heart of logging country, unmarked roads and logging spurs head off in all directions, ensnaring the unprepared. The map used for this description is the *Guide to Forest Land of Southern Vancouver Island*, available from sources listed at the end of the hike.

For the route least likely to flatten your tires, plan to hike from the southern trailhead. From Lake Cowichan, follow South Shore Road to Caycuse and turn left onto the McClure Mainline. Shortly past McClure Lake take the left fork in the road, known as Glad Lake Mainline, and continue heading directly south. Take the next two rights and follow Glad Lake West to where it ends near the park boundary.

From Port Alberni, follow the directions given under Carmanah Valley (see Hike 39) to the Caycuse River Bridge. Turn left onto West Haddon/Carmanah Mainline and follow the next fork to the left. This will be the Walbran Mainline. Follow the Walbran Mainline to a junction with the Glad Lake Mainline. Turn right and proceed as above.

The hike: In 1995 B.C. Parks expanded Carmanah Pacific Provincial Park to include the Lower Walbran Valley. At that time they launched the lengthy

Old-Growth Forests

British Columbia has stands of mature forest ranging in age from 300 to 1,000 years. The definition of *old-growth forest* varies depending on who is doing the defining. In general, however, an unlogged forest where the majority of trees are more than 250 years old is considered an old-growth forest.

process of evaluating existing trails in the park and deciding which to maintain. Currently a number of not-for-profit groups organize volunteer trail-building crews to provide access to old-growth stands in the Walbran Valley, some of which are not part of the park. Trails and camping locations are therefore subject to change. For more information on volunteering or taking a guided hike, contact the Carmanah Forestry Society (see contact information at the end of this description).

From the south trailhead, a number of short day hikes exist in the region of Walbran Creek. Volunteer trail builders recently completed a two- to three-hour loop encompassing Castle Grove—a grove that includes one red cedar with a diameter of almost 5 meters—and Fletcher Falls, although the Bridge Over Troubled Walbran is not yet passable during high-water season. The path directly upstream follows the creek to the falls past a number of prime camping spots. Special features en route to Anderson Lake include Giggling Spruce campsite and Maxine's Tree, one of the largest Sitkas in this part of the valley. Anderson Lake also offers gravel bar camping and the Burled Cedar, another great photo opportunity.

Although volunteers blazed a path from Anderson Lake to Haddon 1000 logging road, this route is extremely difficult and requires solid navigation skills and the willingness to scale deadfall. An alternative is the route to Botley and Auger Lakes, a steep climb up a valley filled with Sitka giants and western red cedar.

Key points (km)

0.0 Start at the southern trailhead off Glad Lake West heading upstream.

0.7 The trail reaches Fletcher Falls.

0.9 The trail reaches Emerald Pond.

1.1 The trail crosses the creek on the Bridge Over Troubled Walbran. Immediately following the bridge is a junction. Turn left. (For Castle Grove, turn right and walk 300 meters.)

2.2 Big Log Junction.

Left from Big Log Junction:

2.5 The trail reaches Maxine's Tree, which is almost 80 meters tall.

2.9 The trail crosses the creek via a logjam.

3.4 The trail reaches Anderson Lake and good camping on the gravel bar.

A "slip-proof" log crossing offers an alternative to the old cable car formerly located in the Walbran Valley.

3.9   The trail moves around the lake and reaches the Burled Cedar.

4.5   The trail crosses a creek.

5.1   The trail crosses another creek.

5.5   The trail reaches the Quintuplets, followed by another campsite.

6.8   The trail reaches Perfection Camp and Haddon 1000.

Right from Big Log Junction:

4.3   The trail reaches a creek crossing and continues climbing up the valley.

5.8   The trail reaches a campsite on Auger Lake.

7.0   The trail reaches the end of Botley Lake and logging road access.

☎ Trail Contacts

B.C. Parks: Web site wlapwww.gov.bc.
ca/bcparks.
Carmanah Forestry Society, 1431
Richardson Street, Victoria, BC V8S
1R1; phone (250) 381–1141.
TimberWest Forest Information Office,
3–4890 Rutherford Road, Nanaimo, BC
V9T 4Z4; phone (250) 729–3766.
Ministry of Forests, South Island
Forest District, 4885 Cherry Creek
Road, Port Alberni, BC V9Y 8E9; phone
(250) 731–3000; fax (250) 731–3010;
e-mail Forests.SouthIslandDistrict
Office@gems3.gov.B.C..ca.

$ Fees/Permits

No fees or permits required.

❓ Local Information

Cowichan Tourism Association, 25

Canada Avenue, Duncan, BC V9L 1T3;
phone (250) 715–0709; fax (250)
715–0710; Web site www.cowichan.bc.
ca; e-mail tourism@cowichan.bc.ca.
Alberni Valley Visitor Info Center, Site
215, C-10, R.R. 2, Port Alberni, BC V9Y
7L6; phone (250) 724–6535; fax
(250) 724–6560; Web site www.avcoc.
com; e-mail avcoc@cedar.alberni.net.

◭ Maps/Brochures

NTS Map 92 C/10.
Carmanah Walbran Provincial Park
brochure.
South and Central Vancouver Island Rec-
reation Map (Carmanah Forestry Society).
Guide to Forest Land of Southern
Vancouver Island (Lake Cowichan
Combined Fire Organization).
Recreation and Logging Road Guide
(Weyerhauser).

41

Clayoquot Valley Witness Trail

*This rugged hike from the Kennedy River Valley through the Clayoquot River watershed
leads to the beautiful meadows of Norgar Lake. It includes views of the rock slide that created Spires Lake as well as alpine meadows and many tricky creek crossings. Hikers on
this trail should be in excellent condition and accustomed to navigating routes with topographic maps and a compass. A decrepit boardwalk presents a challenge for the first kilometer or so. For those with extra time, plan to hike the extension from Norgar Lake to
the spectacular waterfalls located in the Clayoquot River Valley.*

Distance: 10 kilometers.
Approximate hiking time: 6 hours one-way.
Difficulty: Difficult to Norgar Lake. Beyond
Norgar the trail is so overgrown and poorly
marked that only the most determined of bush-

whackers should attempt it.
Type of hike: The way to Lower Solstice Lake is
a moderate climb and scramble over a trail
clogged with the unusable remains of a boardwalk. From here you proceed from lake to lake

Clayoquot Valley Witness Trail

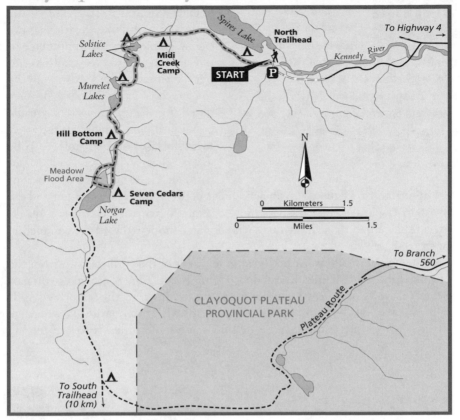

through subalpine areas before descending to the forest floor for the final leg to Norgar Lake.
Elevation gain: 100 meters.
Best season: August to September. Snow stays on the valley floor well into June or July.
Land status: This trail traverses unprotected land between Clayoquot Arm Provincial Park and Clayoquot Plateau Provincial Park.

Finding the trailhead: The north and most accessible trailhead is located off Highway 4, approximately 45 kilometers west of Port Alberni, just beyond Sutton Pass summit. From here it is a further 7 kilometers from the highway on Upper Kennedy Logging Road to your starting point. There are three entrances to this road in the kilometer and a half following the Sutton summit sign. The logging road is not maintained, and you will be required to walk at least a part of this distance to the trailhead. Be on the lookout for bears, which frequent areas near the Kennedy River.

The hike: At the same time that protestors were blocking logging trucks in the now infamous Clayoquot Sound protests of 1993, hearty volunteers were also

The Tla-o-qui-aht, Ahousaht, and Hesquiaht First Nations, part of the Nuu-chah-nulth Tribal Council (NTC), are the aboriginal owners of Clayoquot Sound. Treaty negotiations between the federal and provincial governments and the Nuu-chah-nulth began in 1995 and are still taking place.

building Clayoquot Valley Witness Trail to provide access to stands of ancient rain forest. While the endeavor contributed to shaping public opinion on the importance of old-growth forests, the trail has not been maintained and exists only by the grace of hikers' boots. Be prepared for heavy rains, changeable conditions, and rapidly rising water levels in lakes and streams. Also be aware that Witness Trail passes through Tla-o-qui-aht First Nations traditional territory thanks to an agreement between the Tla-o-qui-aht and the Western Canada Wilderness Committee. Names etched in boardwalk planks are a testament to those individuals who donated money toward the completion of the trail.

The northern and most traversable segment of the trail rises up from the clear-cut that ends Upper Kennedy Logging Road. This route takes you past beautiful views of Spires Lake before plunging down to the water's edge. It is in this section that you must come to grips with the boardwalk wreckage littered across the trail. Assume that it is unusable unless you are feeling brave.

Spires Lake was home to the first camp of volunteer trailbuilders responsible for building the Clayoquot Valley Witness Trail.

Protest!

Between July and November 1993, 12,000 people came to Clayoquot Sound to protest logging activity in the area's pristine rain forests. More than 900 blockaders were arrested near the Kennedy River Bridge, the largest act of civil disobedience in Canadian history.

The trail skirts the edge of Spires Lake before turning away for the climb up out of the Kennedy River Valley. The way up is mostly under cover, but it's a rough 200-meter climb before you finally emerge to views of Needle Mountain and other surrounding peaks. It is here that you cross into the headwaters of the Clayoquot River Valley.

Past the Solstice Lakes you begin your descent back into the forest canopy. There are ropes present at some awkward sections of trail, but these should be treated with caution. Test them before you risk using them; some time has passed since they were installed. It's also worth noting that the presence of boardwalk is mercifully absent from this point on, but that doesn't make the hike any easier.

Glimpses can be seen of the Murrelet Lakes as you wind past and plunge to the bottom of Gorge Hill. The waterfalls here afford a bit of relaxation before the final leg of the hike. The trail to Norgar Lake is relatively flat, following a floodplain to the lake itself. If you attempt this hike early or late in the season, you may find that the route beyond Norgar is blocked by water. Backtracking 500 meters from Seven Cedars Camp will bring you to the high-water trail, which also provides access to the southern portions of Witness Trail. In late summer, waters recede from the eastern portions of the lake to expose scented meadows of mint and wildflowers.

The trail beyond Norgar is very difficult and is neither maintained nor well marked. Only those with backcountry experience should attempt it. There are, however, some sights that you won't want to miss. A day hike from Norgar Lake provides access to the stunning waterfalls plunging to the Clayoquot River below, in addition to unmatched views of the valley. The trail descends in a series of switchbacks beside the falls before crossing the river on a tremendous log-fall bridge. For truly enormous trees, look here on the valley floor.

Key points (km)

0.0 Start at the trailhead located at the end of Upper Kennedy Logging Road. The trail ascends immediately over the wreckage of a (brief) former clear-cut.

1.0 The trail reaches the site of a former trail builder's camp and Spires Lake.

3.5 The trail reaches Midi Creek Camp.

5.0 The trail reaches Solstice Camp on the north end of Lower Solstice Lake.

5.2 The trail reaches Upper Solstice Lake.

7.5	The trail reaches Murrelet Camp on the first of Murrelet Lakes.
8.8	The trail reaches Hill Bottom Camp.
9.6	The trail forks. Continue straight on for Seven Cedars Camp.
10.1	The trail reaches Norgar Lake and Seven Cedars Camp. Camping on the sensitive meadows just north of Norgar Lake is discouraged.

Options: Determined bushwhackers have the option of hooking up with a route through Clayoquot Plateau Provincial Park. This difficult route begins at the end of Branch 560, a spur off Upper Kennedy Logging Road, and traverses the plateau to meet up with Witness Trail south of Norgar Lake.

Hike Information

📞 Local Information

B.C. Forest Service, Port Alberni District Office: phone (250) 731–3000. **Tla-o-qui-aht First Nations,** P.O. Box 18, Tofino, BC V0R 2Z0; phone (250) 725–3233. **Western Canada Wilderness Committee**, Head Office, 227 Abbott Street, Vancouver, BC V6B 2K7; phone (604) 683–8220 or (800) 661–WILD.

💲 Fees/Permits

No fees or permits required.

Maps/Brochures

NTS Maps 92 F/3, 92 F/6. Clayoquot Valley Witness Trail Map and Recreation Guide (Western Canada Wilderness Committee).

Wild Pacific Trail

This relatively new seaside trail begins in the town of Ucluelet and follows the Island's west coast. Still in the works, a section of the trail temporarily parallels some of the town's roads to link up with an extension at Big Beach. The trail also includes views of Barkley Sound and the Broken Islands Group to the east, and the open Pacific to the south and west. Segments feature old-growth thickets and a glimpse into the history of Ucluelet as the trail winds its way around the Amphitrite Lighthouse.

Distance: 8.5 kilometers.
Approximate hiking time: 3 to 5 hours.
Difficulty: Easy.

Type of hike: Wild Side Heritage Trail is mostly a gravel path with some sections of boardwalk and stairs.
Elevation gain: 15 meters. Some light to mod-

Wild Pacific Trail

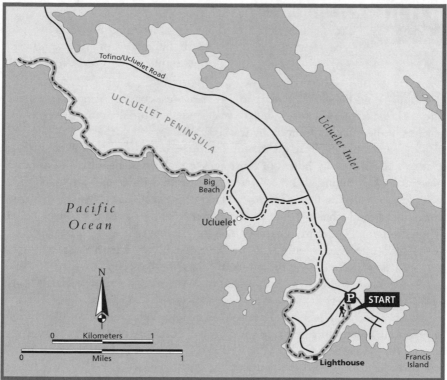

erate inclines. This trail is generally at sea level with no significant elevation gains.

Best season: Year-round. Most hike the trail in spring, summer, and fall, though winter hikes are good opportunities for storm-watching.

Land status: A combination of park, private land, and forest land reserve.

Finding the trailhead: From Port Alberni, take Highway 4 to the west coast of Vancouver Island and follow signs to Ucluelet, located just south of Pacific Rim National Park (Long Beach Unit). Once in Ucluelet, you can access the trail by one of several trailheads, all of which are well signed. The lower portion of the trail, also known as Phase One, is a loop beginning at the southern end of town. Drive 9.7 kilometers from the turnoff onto Tofino/Ucluelet Road until you reach the junction of Peninsula and Coast Guard Roads. The trailhead parking lot begins at this junction.

Phases Three and Four of the trail, also known as the Big Beach Extension, extend from Big Beach Park to the bike path just outside Ucluelet. Access this portion of the trail via Phase One and a short, in-town connector, or start hiking at the Pacific Rim Highway Trailhead 2 kilometers north of Ucluelet. Look for a sign on the west side just before a bend in the road, approximately 7.7

kilometers from the turnoff.

A third starting point is possible using the He-Tin-Kis Park Trailhead, approximately 200 meters north by road from the southernmost trailhead for Wild Pacific Trail.

The hike: Wild Pacific Trail skirts the rugged west coast of Vancouver Island, where the ancient rain forest meets the headlands, tidal pools, and pristine beaches of the Pacific Ocean. The trail is a wide, gravel surfaced walking path with only light to moderate inclines and some sections of boardwalk and stairs, so it can be enjoyed by hikers of most ages and abilities. Featuring panoramic views of Barkley Sound and the Broken Islands of Pacific Rim National Park, it meanders beneath the forest canopy and along a spectacular coastline abundant with seabirds and whales. From the trail, hikers may also see deer, black bears, fishing boats, and ocean freighters. Perfect for photography and storm-watching, the Wild Pacific Trail is truly "Life on the Edge." Nature enthusiasts may spot gray whales offshore during their annual migration between late February and late May. Other wildlife commonly seen from the trail includes seals, sea lions, mink, and river otters.

Wild Pacific Trail is a seven-phase trail system. While the current trail follows 8.5 kilometers of the Island's west coast, plans are in place to extend the hike all the way to Pacific Rim National Park for a total of almost 20 kilometers. The trail will eventually meet up with Half Moon Bay, just below Florencia Bay in the Long Beach Unit of the park.

Throughout history Ucluelet has provided shelter from the storm-tossed waters of the Pacific Ocean. Until the early 1870s Ucluelet was a First Nations village. During the height of the sealing era, in the 1880s, European settlers came to the area to establish a trading post and acquire timber holdings. Still later, in 1903, a whaling station was established on Barkley Sound. Built in 1906, the first Amphitrite Lighthouse was a small wooden tower erected at the edge of the forest. When a tidal wave swept it away in 1912, the current lighthouse was built as a replacement.

The first 2.5 kilometers of the hike consist of a gravel-surfaced trail with several moderate inclines, beginning at the southern edge of Ucluelet and passing Amphitrite Lighthouse and the Canadian Coastguard Station. A complete loop is possible by connecting to the He-Tin-Kis Park boardwalk trail. While the entire loop takes approximately an hour, shorter sections of twenty to thirty minutes are also possible.

Phase Two of the trail, from kilometer 2.5 to kilometer 4.5, follows a temporary route through town. Walking through the town of Ucluelet, take the sidewalk along Peninsula Road and gravel shoulder along Marine Drive. Follow the gravel road through the brush to Big Beach Park.

From 4.5 to 8.5 kilometers is a longer and steeper part of the trail that

Picturesque tidal pools along the rocky shoreline near Ucluelet provide homes for a wide array of intertidal life.

begins at Big Beach in Ucluelet, following the rugged coastline and rain forest to the north, ending at the Pacific Rim Highway. From there hikers can walk along the "bike path" back to town.

Options: For an extended walk, take in the He-Tin-Kis Park boardwalk trail located in Phase One of Wild Pacific Trail.

Hike Information

 Trail Contact
Ucluelet Chamber of Commerce, 100 Main Street, Ucluelet, BC V0R 3A0; phone (250) 726–4641; fax (250) 726–4611; Web site www.wildpacifictrail.com; e-mail info@uclueletinfo.com.

Fees/Permits
No fees or permits required.

Local Information
Tofino–Long Beach Chamber of Commerce, P. O. Box 249, Tofino, BC V0R 2Z0; phone (250) 725–3414; fax (250) 725–3296; Web site www.island.net/~tofino; e-mail tofino@island.net.

Gold Mine Trail

This level path follows Lost Shoe Creek to picturesque Florencia Bay. The surrounding forest is an enjoyable place to visit in autumn when the leaves are changing color. Suitable for all ages, this trail also traces the history of placer mining claims in the area. Take along a picnic lunch for a picturesque rest stop on the sandy beaches of the windswept Pacific.

Distance: 1.5 kilometers.
Approximate hiking time: 20 minutes.
Difficulty: Easy.
Type of hike: A flat, broad path with no boardwalk that meanders through dark forest around and behind Florencia Bay.
Elevation gain: No significant elevation gains.
Best season: Year-round.
Land status: National park reserve.

Finding the trailhead: From Ucluelet, drive west to the Pacific Rim National Park Reserve Highway Information Center, located approximately 3 kilometers from the Port Alberni turnoff. (This center may be relocated to the Highway 4 junction as early as 2003.) Here you can purchase a park access permit, which is required for all vehicles stopping in the park—even those registered with Green Point Campground. The trailhead is located a further 1 kilometer west and is marked by yellow road signs on the Pacific Rim Highway that indicate GOLD MINE TRAIL.

The hike: The trail follows Lost Shoe Creek through red alder and Douglas fir

Gold Mine Trail

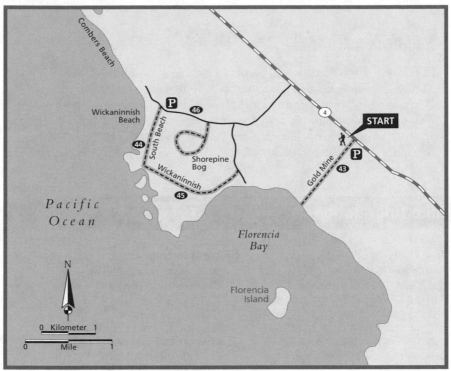

forest and affords a good view of the Island coast. Look for signs on the trail that explain the forest environment and the human history of the area. A rusty old wreck from a mining dredge sits on the creek bank, marking the site of small mining operations in the early 1900s. Claims were staked in 1899 when gold was found on the sandy beach. Story has it that more than $20,000 in gold was taken from the beach at that time. During this mini gold rush, those eager to strike it rich panned for gold in the sands opposite the trail to the beach.

Years later the trail was widened for logging purposes. Native amabilis fir, red cedar, and hemlock were cleared and replaced by Douglas fir and Sitka spruce. Since then a number of the original tree species have reestablished themselves. The green archway at the lower end of the trail is proof of the lushness and newfound diversity of

Tidbit Approximately 250 species of birds have been identified within Pacific Rim National Park Reserve and bordering areas. The best bird-watching times coincide with the seasonal migration of the many thousands of birds that stop en route to visit the park's vast and varied shorelines.

this forest. In the future, interpretive displays will highlight First Nations activities in the area.

Nuu-chah-nulth Trail

In fall 2003 Parks Canada will construct a trail connecting the Gold Mine Trail to the Florencia Bay beach access. A loop will be created from the Wickaninnish Center parking lot to the Gold Mine Trail parking lot and will include Wickaninnish Trail and a segment of South Beach Trail. The entire loop will be renamed Nuu-chah-nulth Trail. A shuttle service will transport hikers between parking lots.

Hike Information

Trail Contacts

Pacific Rim National Park Reserve: (250) 726–7721 or, seasonally, (250) 726–4212. For all other inquiries, contact the Administration Office, Pacific Rim National Park Reserve, Box 280, Ucluelet, BC V0R 3A0; Web site www.parkscan.harbour.com/pacrim/; e-mail pacriminfo@pc.gc.ca.

Fees/Permits

$8.00 per day for park access.

Local Information

Tofino–Long Beach Chamber of Commerce, P. O. Box 249, Tofino, BC V0R 2Z0; phone (250) 725–3414; fax (250) 725–3296; Web site www.island.net/~tofino; e-mail tofino@island.net.

Ucluelet Chamber of Commerce, 100 Main Street, Ucluelet, BC V0R 3A0; phone (250) 726–4641; fax (250) 726–4611; Web site www.uclueletinfo.com; e-mail info@uclueletinfo.com.

Maps/Brochures

Long Beach Unit Trail Guide (Parks Canada).

44 South Beach Trail

The trail affords stunning views of glorious beaches and crashing surf. A stone's throw from the trail is Lismer Beach, named for Arthur Lismer, one of the famous Group of Seven painters who spent many summers immortalizing Canada's wilderness. Lismer Beach is a good place to explore tidal pools at low tide. Take along a pocket identification guide to learn more about the area's rich variety of intertidal marine life.

South Beach Trail

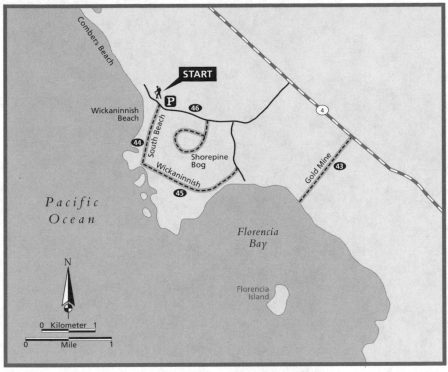

Distance: 0.7 kilometer.
Approximate hiking time: 20 minutes.
Difficulty: Easy.
Type of hike: Boardwalk and gravel path wind through oceanside fir forest.
Elevation gain: No significant elevation gains, though there is a ramp up to the Wickaninnish Trail intersection and stairs down to South Beach.
Best season: All seasons, although boardwalks may be slippery during the winter.
Land status: National park reserve.

Finding the trailhead: From Ucluelet, follow the signs on the Pacific Rim Highway to Wickaninnish Beach. Turn left at Wickaninnish Road and park next to the Wickaninnish Center, remembering to purchase a parking permit at the yellow machine located in the parking lot. Permits are required for all vehicles in Pacific Rim National Park Reserve, even those registered with Green Point Campground. Follow the gradual paved service road up the hill and past the Wickaninnish Center. A paved trail starts behind the building.

There were an estimated 9,000 people living in the area now known as Pacific Rim National Park Reserve when Europeans first arrived. Today six groups remain: the Tseshaht, Ucluelet, Tla-o-qui-aht, Huu-ay-aht, Ditidaht, and Pacheedaht.

The hike: This trail begins as a paved path winding through a forest of Sitka spruce. After a short distance, a gravel pathway alternates with a boardwalk across the Ucluelet First Nation Kwisitis Reserve. Other paths lead off toward sandy coves or lookout points enclosed by rocky bluffs, offering the perfect chance to discover marine life or to view the beach from above. Marine creatures such as sea anemones, goose barnacles, and hermit crabs are found in the tidal pools or attached to rocky shores. There is also a good variety of marine plant life including sea palms, kelp beds, Turkish towel, and sea lettuce. In the forest, giant Sitka spruce and western hemlocks create a majestic sight with the ocean as a backdrop. Watch for the trail's carved log bridges and many stairs.

At the far end of Lismer Beach, the boardwalk ascends over the bluff toward South Beach. From here you can see views along Long Beach toward Schooner Cove. The path is lined with salal, salmonberry, and blackberry. Due to the availability of wild berries, bears may be active on paths during summer and early fall. Watch for park signs indicating BEAR IN AREA.

At the top of the next hill, Wickaninnish Trail leading to Florencia Bay veers to the left. Continue to the right along the boardwalk sections where reindeer moss clings to aging snags. South Beach marks the end of the boardwalk section of the trail. Be careful of swells if venturing onto the craggy rocks in winter. To the right, waves force water into the rocky bluffs. Local residents have named this place Edge of the Silver Thunder.

To the left, a walk along South Beach leads to a sheltered area. You may see harbor seals and otters basking in the cove. In fair weather, rounded cobblestones edging the shoreline make warm places for a well-earned rest.

Hike Information

Trail Contacts
Pacific Rim National Park Reserve:
(250) 726–7721 or, seasonally, (250) 726–4212. For all other inquiries, contact the Administration Office, Pacific Rim National Park Reserve, Box 280, Ucluelet, BC V0R 3A0; Web site www.parkscan.harbour.com/pacrim/; e-mail pacriminfo@pc.gc.ca.

Fees/Permits
$8.00 per day for park access.

Local Information
Tofino–Long Beach Chamber of Commerce, P. O. Box 249, Tofino, BC V0R 2Z0; phone (250) 725–3414; fax (250) 725–3296; Web site www.island. net/~tofino; e-mail tofino@island.net.
Ucluelet Chamber of Commerce, 100 Main Street, Ucluelet, BC V0R 3A0; phone (250) 726–4641; fax (250) 726–4611; Web site www.ucluelet info.com; e-mail info@uclueletinfo.com.

Maps/Brochures
Long Beach Unit Trail Guide (Parks Canada).

Trees like this western red cedar on the South Beach Trail often dwarf the hiker.

Wickaninnish Trail

One of the longest trails in the Long Beach Unit of Pacific Rim National Park, Wickaninnish Trail follows a portion of the original Tofino-Ucluelet land route. Passing through a variety of ecosystems including beaches, forest, and wetlands, the trail sports the old corduroy-surfaced road beneath encroaching layers of sphagnum moss. Petroglyphs showing five animal figures can be found on a rock face near the end of Quisitis Point. Follow the cliffs around the end of the point to find them.

Distance: 2.5 kilometers.
Approximate hiking time: 40 minutes.
Difficulty: Easy to moderate.
Type of hike: This trail stretches to Quisitis Point connecting Long Beach to Florencia (Wreck) Bay. A portion of Wickaninnish Trail was the principal

road between Ucluelet and Tofino until 1942. Some of the cedar poles laid across the trail to form the corduroy road are still visible.
Elevation gain: No significant elevation gains.
Best season: Year-round.
Land status: National park reserve.

Finding the trailhead: This trail has two access points. From Ucluelet, follow the Pacific Rim Highway to Wickaninnish Road. Taking a second left at the Florencia Bay sign will lead you to the parking area. For Long Beach, take the first left fork off South Beach Trail located behind the Wickaninnish Center (see the description of South Beach, Hike 44).

The hike: Wickaninnish Bay was named for a Nuu-chah-nulth chief and leader of the Tla-o-qui-aht people in the 1800s. Because Wickaninnish Trail takes you from Long Beach to Florencia (Wreck) Bay, expect to see spectacular shoreline views at both the start and end of your journey. Between these

Vancouver Island's Daily Cycle

A typical twenty-four-hour cycle on Vancouver Island includes two low tides and two high tides. These tides are unequal in height and are dependent on the gravitational forces of the moon (and, to a lesser extent, the sun). Intertidal marine life (creatures that live between high and low tide) have many special adaptations that enable them to live both above and below the water. Typically you will find them tucked into crevices or shadows at low tide, or hiding out in tidal pools or beneath the sand. Others, like barnacles, will stay where they are, closing up tight and waiting out the tidal shift. The best time to see marine life is in and around the lowest tide. This is also often the best time to hike, when the ocean pulls back to reveal flat, firm beaches.

Wickaninnish Trail

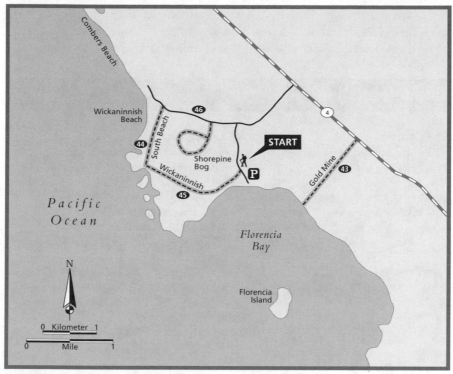

Steps down to Florencia Bay provide easy access to the surf-tossed beaches of Pacific Rim National Park.

ocean vistas is a rain forest trail taking you past small ravines, creeks and rivers, bogs, and cliffs. Large coniferous trees such as the western hemlock, western red cedar, and Douglas fir dominate this dense forest. Trees of various ages—some up to 1,200 years old—mosses and lichens, and a lush canopy and undergrowth characterize the coastal temperate rain forest.

Hike Information

Trail Contacts

Pacific Rim National Park Reserve: (250) 726–7721 or, seasonally, (250) 726–4212. For all other inquiries, contact the Administration Office, Pacific Rim National Park Reserve, Box 280, Ucluelet, BC V0R 3A0; Web site www.parkscan.harbour.com/pacrim/; e-mail pacriminfo@pc.gc.ca.

Fees/Permits

$8.00 per day for park access.

Local Information

Tofino–Long Beach Chamber of Commerce, P. O. Box 249, Tofino, BC V0R 2Z0; phone (250) 725–3414; fax (250) 725–3296; Web site www.island.net/~tofino; e-mail tofino@island.net.

Ucluelet Chamber of Commerce, 100 Main Street, Ucluelet, BC V0R 3A0; phone (250) 726–4641; fax (250) 726–4611; Web site www. uclueletinfo.com; e-mail info@uclueletinfo.com.

Maps/Brochures

Long Beach Unit Trail Guide (Parks Canada).

46

Shorepine Bog

This short, wheelchair-accessible boardwalk passes through a Dr. Seuss landscape to view life in a coastal bog. Characteristic flora includes the shore, or lodgepole, pine; low-growing cranberry; and the carnivorous sundew. Take this self-guided nature hike using the bilingual interpretive brochures available at the trailhead and learn about the formation of this unique landscape.

Distance: 0.8-kilometer loop.
Approximate strolling time: 30 minutes.
Difficulty: Easy.
Type of hike: Flat maintained boardwalk.

Elevation gain: No significant elevation gains.
Best season: All seasons, although winter rains may make for a slippery boardwalk.
Land status: National park reserve.

Shorepine Bog

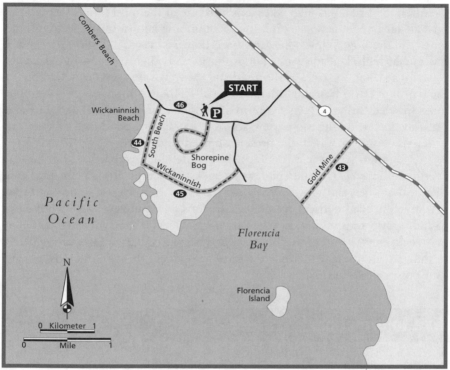

Finding the trailhead: From Ucluelet, take the Pacific Rim Highway to Wickaninnish Beach Road and continue 0.3 kilometer past the Florencia Beach turnoff. Follow the sign to Bog Trail. A park access permit is required and can be obtained on site from one of the park's permit-dispensing machines.

The hike: A bog is a very old lake with a water table that is more than 30 centimeters below the surface. At some point in the lake's history, moss began encroaching on the water's surface, forming a dense mat on top of which other plants could grow. Eventually the lake became an area with no open water, low in the types of nutrients typically needed by forest plants. Due to the reclamation and infilling of old bog lands, Canadian bogs are becoming a rarity. One result of this loss is the decrease in the water-holding capacity of land. Without bogs to hold back rains and floodwaters, some watersheds experience increased sil-

Tidbit In some parts of Europe, bogs or heaths were the haunts of society's outcasts. These bog livers became known as "bogeymen" or "heathens."

tation of their creeks and rivers. Silty waterways disrupt the life cycle of salmon, a keystone species of Vancouver Island's forest ecosystems.

Although brief, this hike takes you into one of the most unique landscapes on Vancouver Island. Shore pine trees, commonly known inland as lodgepole pines, fill the bog. While some are more than 300 years old, most are only a few meters high. Due to a lack of phosphorus and other nutrients in the acidic, waterlogged soil, the trees are stunted and slow growing, often resembling (in the words of Parks Canada) "a large broccoli." About 400 years ago sphagnum moss invaded this area, taking root in a hardpan of minerals and decay from a previous forest. As the moss grew and the water table continued to rise, the original forest gave way to the present stunted landscape.

As you wind your way through the bog, watch for crowberry, Labrador tea, evergreen huckleberry, and sundew—a sticky red carnivorous plant that eats flies, mosquitoes, and ants. Because bog soil is low in nitrogen, some plants get this much-needed nutrient from a carnivorous diet. Sundew uses its red hairs to hold down trapped insects while it slowly digests them. Although the bog may seem empty of other wildlife, deer and bears frequent the area at night and in the early morning. Their narrow trails are evident through the moss at various points along the hike.

Hike Information

Trail Contacts
Pacific Rim National Park Reserve: (250) 726–7721 or, seasonally, (250) 726–4212. For all other inquiries, contact the Administration Office, Pacific Rim National Park Reserve, Box 280, Ucluelet, BC V0R 3A0; Web site www.parkscan.harbour.com/pacrim/; e-mail pacriminfo@pc.gc.ca.

Fees/Permits
$8.00 per day for park access.

Local Information
Tofino–Long Beach Chamber of Commerce, P. O. Box 249, Tofino, BC V0R 2Z0; phone (250) 725–3414; fax (250) 725–3296; Web site www.island.net/~tofino; e-mail tofino@island.net.
Ucluelet Chamber of Commerce, 100 Main Street, Ucluelet, BC V0R 3A0; phone (250) 726–4641; fax (250) 726–4611; Web site www.ucluelet info.com; e-mail info@uclueletinfo.com.

Maps/Brochures
Long Beach Unit Trail Guide (Parks Canada).
Shore Pine Bog interpretive brochure.

Rainforest Figure Eight

This figure-eight double loop circles through impressive examples of western red cedar, western hemlock, and amabilis fir, forming what scientists call the climax rain forest community. Carpeted in thick layers of hanging moss, this old-growth forest supports a diversity of plants and animals, including trees dating back hundreds of years. Watch for songbirds in the upper canopy and salmon spawning in Sandhill Creek. Interpretive signs on both trails provide descriptions of old-growth forest cycles (Loop A) and forest structure and inhabitants (Loop B).

Distance: 2-kilometer double loop.
Approximate hiking time: 40 minutes.
Difficulty: Easy.
Type of hike: Well-maintained gravel path and boardwalk.

Elevation gain: No significant elevation gains. Some of the stair sets may be demanding for the elderly.
Best season: All seasons, although winter rains may make for a slippery boardwalk.
Land status: National park reserve.

Rainforest Figure Eight

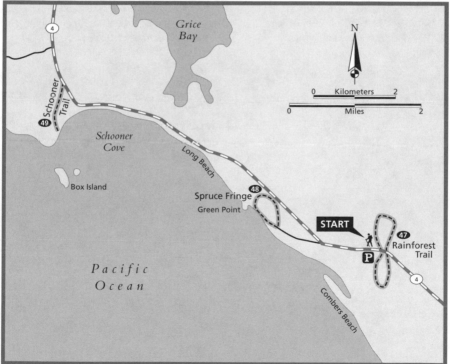

Finding the trailhead: From Ucluelet, follow the Pacific Rim Highway west to Pacific Rim National Park Reserve. Locate the parking area 6.4 kilometers past the Park Highway Information Center, where signs indicate trailheads on both sides of the highway. A park access permit is required and can be obtained on site from one of the park's permit-dispensing machines.

The hike: Another brief but lovely hike through west coast rain forest, perfect for families and individuals looking for a taste of giant cedars, mossy carpets, and trees older than European settlement on Vancouver Island. Loop A follows first a gravel path, then a series of boardwalks, stairs, and bridges through various levels of the rain forest, winding around fallen giants, new seedlings, and spreading boughs. Because of the relatively popular nature of this trail and its narrow boardwalk, we suggest following the trail arrows around the loop to prevent traffic jams with oncoming hikers.

Hike Information

Trail Contacts

Pacific Rim National Park Reserve: (250) 726–7721 or, seasonally, (250) 726–4212. For all other inquiries, contact the Administration Office, Pacific Rim National Park Reserve, Box 280, Ucluelet, BC V0R 3A0; Web site www.parkscan. harbour.com/pacrim/; e-mail pacriminfo@pc.gc.ca.

Fees/Permits

$8.00 per day for park access.

Local Information

Tofino–Long Beach Chamber of Commerce, P. O. Box 249, Tofino, BC V0R 2Z0; phone (250) 725–3414; fax (250) 725–3296; Web site www.island.net/~tofino; e-mail tofino@island.net.

Ucluelet Chamber of Commerce, 100 Main Street, Ucluelet, BC V0R 3A0; phone (250) 726–4641; fax (250) 726–4611; Web site www.uclueletinfo.com; e-mail info@uclueletinfo.com.

Maps/Brochures

Long Beach Unit Trail Guide (Parks Canada).

Spruce Fringe

Take an easy stroll through a forest on the edge to view a community of Vancouver Island's Sitka spruce. Here these impressive giants reach heights of 50 to 90 meters and dominate a forest hunkered down against the tumult of the Pacific. At their most exposed, the Sitka spruce form a distinctive "krummholz"—a dense and stunted thicket that protects the inner reaches of the forest from the wrath of dramatic weather. Highlights of the hike include spruce fringe tunnels, interpretive signs, the buried bones of an ancient whale, and trees up to 800 years old.

Distance: 1.5-kilometer loop.
Approximate hiking time: 35 minutes.
Difficulty: Easy.
Type of hike: A well-maintained boardwalk with interpretive displays.

Elevation gain: No significant elevation gain. Some of the stair sets may be demanding for the elderly.
Best season: All seasons, but winter weather can make for a slippery boardwalk.
Land status: National park reserve.

Finding the trailhead: From Ucluelet, follow the Pacific Rim Highway west to Pacific Rim National Park Reserve. Locate the parking lot at the western end of the Combers Beach day-use area. Follow park signs to the Spruce Fringe Trailhead. A park access permit is required and can be obtained on site from one of the park's permit-dispensing machines.

The hike: A brief but interesting (and awe-inspiring) walk through mature forest bordering the Pacific. Watch for impenetrable thickets of young spruce and salal forming on the water's edge, moss-hung branches overhead, as well as fallen giants providing nutrients for future forests. The boardwalk provides beach access through a side trail of compact, bushy vegetation, and eventually crosses over the bones of a whale beached in a previous century.

Bull Kelp

On the surf-tossed beaches of Pacific Rim Park Reserve, watch for strands of bull kelp *(Nereocystis luetkeana)*, which can grow up to 20 meters. While bull kelp grows intertidally and subtidally in waters up to 20 meters deep, it also dies off in winter and washes ashore during storms, decorating beaches with its long, snakelike stalks.

Spruce Fringe

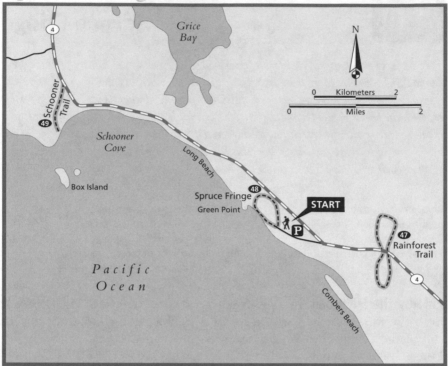

Hike Information

Trail Contacts

Pacific Rim National Park Reserve:
(250) 726–7721 or, seasonally, (250)
726–4212. For all other inquiries, contact the Administration Office, Pacific
Rim National Park Reserve, Box 280,
Ucluelet, BC V0R 3A0; Web site www.
parkscan.harbour.com/pacrim/; e-mail
pacriminfo@pc.gc.ca.

Fees/Permits

$8.00 per day for park access.

Local Information

**Tofino–Long Beach Chamber of
Commerce,** P.O. Box 249, Tofino, BC
V0R 2Z0; phone (250) 725–3414; fax
(250) 725–3296; Web site www.island.
net/~tofino; e-mail tofino@island.net.
Ucluelet Chamber of Commerce, 100
Main Street, Ucluelet, BC V0R 3A0;
phone (250) 726–4641; fax (250)
726–4611; Web site www.ucluelet
info.com; e-mail info@uclueletinfo.com.

Maps/Brochures

Long Beach Unit Trail Guide (Parks
Canada).

Schooner Trail

An easy walk through coastal old-growth forests, this hike winds over level boardwalks and moderate staircases to Schooner Cove and Long Beach. Several examples of giant Sitka spruce are evident along the way and make for cool rest spots on a hot day. This trail ends at an island that is accessible at low tide and home to an abundance of rocky tidal pools. Be sure to consult your tide tables and take care when crossing over the small salmon spawning stream.

Distance: 1.0 kilometer.

Approximate hiking time: 20 minutes one-way.

Difficulty: Moderate.

Type of hike: Maintained boardwalk and soft natural trail.

Elevation gain: No significant elevation gains.

Best season: All seasons, although winter rains make for a slippery boardwalk.

Land status: National park reserve.

Finding the trailhead: From Ucluelet, follow the Pacific Rim Highway west to Pacific Rim National Park Reserve. Locate the parking area on your left 4.8 kilometers north of Green Point Campground. Follow park signs to the Schooner Cove Trailhead. A park access permit is required and can be obtained on site from one of the park's permit-dispensing machines.

Boardwalks in Pacific Rim National Park lead through mature giants and new seedlings to vast sand beaches.

Schooner Trail

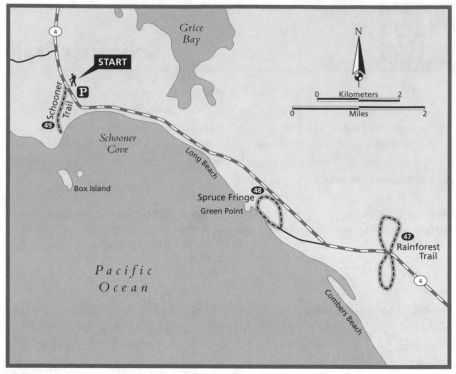

The hike: One of our favorite hikes in upper Pacific Rim National Park Reserve, Schooner Trail winds through mature western red cedar and Douglas fir forests, down to giant examples of Sitka spruce. A boardwalk protects sensitive roots underfoot and provides lookouts and viewing platforms for some of the trail's largest inhabitants. If you are exploring at low tide, we recommend walking to Box Island, accessible at the end of the trail past a short section of sand beach. The island offers excellent opportunities to view inter-

Sitka Spruce

The Sitka spruce *(Picea sitchensis)* is one of British Columbia's largest spruces and is usually found along the Island's west coast.

tidal wildlife living in rocky tidal pools and on rock surfaces. Be sure not to move or disturb wildlife. A few inches in the intertidal zone means life or death to some creatures.

Hike Information

● Trail Contacts
Pacific Rim National Park Reserve: (250) 726–7721 or, seasonally, (250) 726–4212. For all other inquiries, contact the Administration Office, Pacific Rim National Park Reserve, Box 280, Ucluelet, BC V0R 3A0; Web site www. parkscan.harbour.com/pacrim/; e-mail pacriminfo@pc.gc.ca.

● Fees/Permits
$8.00 per day for park access.

● Local Information
Tofino–Long Beach Chamber of Commerce, P. O. Box 249, Tofino, BC V0R 2Z0; phone (250) 725–3414; fax (250) 725–3296; Web site www.island. net/~tofino; e-mail tofino@island.net. **Ucluelet Chamber of Commerce,** 100 Main Street, Ucluelet, BC V0R 3A0; phone (250) 726–4641; fax (250) 726–4611; Web site www.ucluelet info.com; e-mail info@uclueletinfo.com.

● Maps/Brochures
Long Beach Unit Trail Guide (Parks Canada).

50

Nootka Island

This weeklong hike along Nootka Island's west coast includes waterfalls, beaches, rocky headlands, and old-growth forests, as well as a journey back into the origins of British Columbia. Okay, so it's not technically Vancouver Island, but the hike between Louie Bay in the north and Yuquot in the south provides opportunities to view whales, sea otters, and other marine life in a stunning wilderness accessible via Vancouver Island's west coast. Take your binoculars and be prepared for other hikers. This trail is rapidly gaining in popularity.

Distance: Approximately 37 kilometers.
Approximate hiking time: 5 to 7 days.
Difficulty: Though most of the trail is relatively flat, this hike is difficult due to steep sections with ropes and a few obstacle courses involving deadfall and muddy quagmires.

Type of hike: A beach route that follows the rugged shoreline of Nootka Island. A good three-quarters of this hike involves walking the intertidal zone at low tide. Where rocky headlands prevent passage at any time of day, forested trails hacked out by volunteers provide a slippery but good bypass. This is

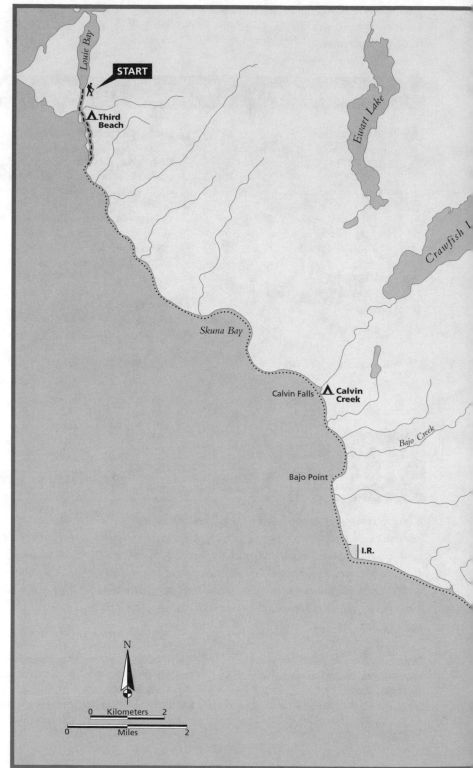

Nootka Island

Louie Bay

START

△ **Third Beach**

Skuna Bay

Calvin Falls △ **Calvin Creek**

Bajo Creek

Bajo Point

I.R.

Ewart Lake

Crawfish L

N

0 Kilometers 2

0 Miles 2

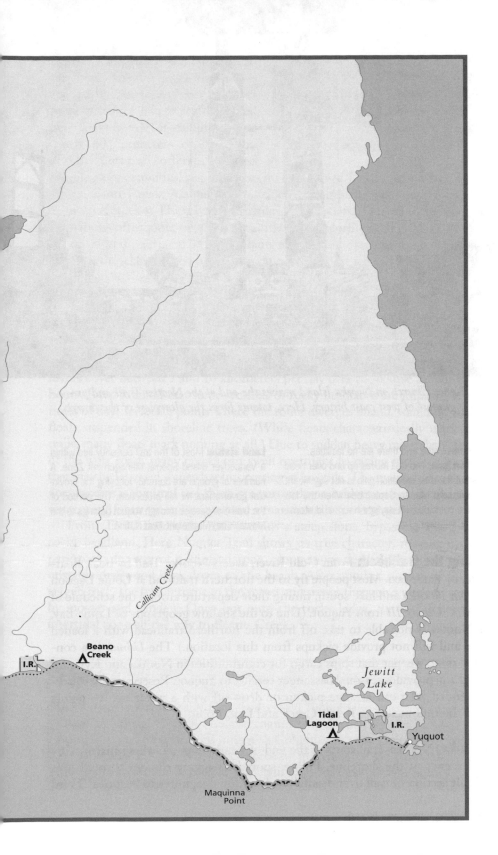

Beano
Creek

Callicum Creek

I.R.

Jewitt
Lake

Tidal
Lagoon

I.R.

Yuquot

Maquinna
Point

1.8   The trail returns to the forest via an inland route. Over the next several hundred meters, the trail pops in and out of the forest several times.

2.2   The trail comes to a junction. Turn right and follow the trail through a fen.

2.9   The trail emerges from the forest onto a cobble beach.

3.5   The trail crosses two minor creeks within 400 meters of one another.

3.9   The trail meets a flat rocky ledge and follows the shoreline.

5.4   The trail crosses another creek.

7.8   Campsites are available on the north side of Skuna Bay by an unnamed creek.

8.0   The trail reaches Skuna Bay. More sandstone provides good opportunities for exploring tidal pools.

10.0   The trail reaches rocky headlands on the south side of Skuna Bay. These are passable at low tide.

12.3   The trail reaches Calvin Creek and Calvin (or Crawfish) Falls. Campsites are available on the south side of the creek.

13.2   The trail crosses two minor creeks within 600 meters of one another.

14.2   The trail reaches Bajo Creek. This is a good spot to watch for sea otters.

15.5   The trail crosses an unnamed creek.

17.3   The land above the high-tide line at Bajo Point is designated First Nations land.

20.0   The trail crosses two minor creeks within 1 kilometer of one another.

23.0   The trail reaches Beano Creek. North of the creek is designated First Nations land. South of the creek is a parcel of privately owned land.

24.7   The trail returns to the forest to bypass rocky headlands.

25.6   The trail emerges from the forest. Within 100 meters is Callicum Creek.

26.3   The trail crosses a minor creek.

28.3   The trail returns to the forest to bypass the rocky headlands of Maquinna Point.

32.9   Turn right on a side trail for a view from Maquinna Point. Rejoin the main trail before continuing ahead.

33.5   The trail forks. Take the right fork to view a series of sea caves and then rejoin the trail to continue.

34.7   The trail reaches a tidal lagoon. Camping is available on the south side of the lagoon, though fresh water is scarce. Above the high-tide line is a parcel of private land.

36.0   Just beyond the rocky shoreline, a small creek offers fresh water. Be aware that this is also near the border of Mowachaht/Muchalaht First Nations land.

37.4   The trail turns left and crosses over a grassy area to the government dock. The Mowachaht/Muchalaht First Nations charge a $5.00-per-person landing fee to visit their historic land and its features.

37.6   The trail reaches the government dock where the M.V. *Uchuck III* picks up passengers for Gold River.

Hike Information

Trail Contacts

I Need to Know the Nootka Trail: www.i-needtoknow.com/nootka.
Air Nootka Ltd., P.O. Box 19, Gold River, BC V0P 1G0; phone (250) 283–2255; fax (250) 283–2256; Web site www.airnootka.com.
Nootka Sound Service (M.V. *Uchuck III*), P.O. Box 57, Gold River, BC V0P 1G0; phone (250) 283–2515; fax (250) 283–7582; Web site www.mvuchuck. com; e-mail info@mvuchuck.com.
Mowachaht/Muchalaht First Nations, A'haminaquus Tourist Center, P.O. Box 459, Gold River, BC V0P 1G0; phone (250) 283–2015; fax (250) 283–2335; toll-free (800) 238–2933; Web site www.yuquot.ca; e-mail info@yuquot.ca.
Maxi's Water Taxi, P.O. Box 1122, Gold River, BC V0P 1G0; phone (250) 283–2282; fax (250) 283–2335.
Ray Williams Water Taxi (Yuquot), P. O. Box 364, Gold River, BC V0P 1G0. VHF Channel 66; call "My Sandy."

Fees/Permits

A $5.00-per-person landing fee is required in addition to transportation costs.

Local Information

Gold River Visitor Info Center, P. O. Box 610, Gold River, BC V0P 1G0; phone (250) 283–2418 or (250) 283–2202; fax (250) 283–7500; Web site www.village.goldriver.bc.ca; e-mail goldriv@island.net.
Department of Fisheries and Oceans: phone (604) 666–2828; Web site www.pac.dfo-mpo.gc.ca.

Maps/Brochures

NTS Map 92 E/10.
Nautical chart 3662.
The Nootka Trail: Walking the Wild West Coast (Federation of B.C. Mountain Clubs).
Yatzmahs Trail brochure (Mowachaht/Muchalaht).
Tide Predictions (Canadian Hydrographic Service, Institute of Ocean Sciences): www-sci.pac.dfo-mpo.gc.ca/charts/Tides/Home_e.htm.
Tide Tables (Fisheries and Oceans Canada): www.lau.chs-shc.dfo-mpo. gc.ca/marees/produits/accueil.htm.

The Art of Hiking

When standing nose to snout with a black bear, you're probably not too concerned with the issue of ethical behavior in the wild. No doubt you're just wetting yourself. But let's be honest. How often are you nose to snout with a black bear? For many of us, a hike into the "wild" means loading up the SUV with everything MEC and driving to a toileted trailhead. Sure, you can mourn how civilized we've become—how GPS units have replaced natural instinct and Gore-Tex, true grit—but the silly gadgets of civilization aside, we have plenty of reason to take pride in how we've matured. With survival now on the back burner, we've begun to reason—and it's about time—that we have a responsibility to protect, no longer just conquer, our wild places; that they, not we, are at risk. So please, do what you can. Now, in keeping with our chronic tendency to reduce everything to a list, here are some rules to remember.

• *Zero impact.* Always leave an area just like you found it—if not better than you found it. Avoid camping in fragile, alpine meadows and along the banks of streams and lakes. If you are not respectfully tracking wildlife, make noise on the trail to alert nearby animals. Stay on trails to preserve threatened and endangered ecosystems rather than shortcutting and causing damage. Refrain from taking souvenirs of your trip such as wildflowers, seashells, and Vancouver Island marmots. Use a lightweight camp stove versus building a wood fire. In backcountry areas, fires should be used only in emergencies. If you must smoke, do so only at rest stops and carry out all cigarette butts. Pack up all of your trash and extra food and carry it out with you. Where no outhouse facilities exist, bury human waste at least 60 meters from water sources and under 15 to 20 centimeters of topsoil, away from paths and campsites. Burn toilet paper when fires are available. Don't bathe with soap (even biodegradable soap) in a lake or stream. Even your body oils (especially if you're wearing sunscreen) can contaminate water sources, so try to take water in a container at least 50 meters from water sources and wash and rinse there. Remember to dump the wastewater away from water sources. Another option is to use prepackaged moistened towels to wipe off sweat and dirt. Do not dump food scraps in streams or creeks no matter how hungry the fish look.

• *Leave no weeds.* Noxious weeds tend to outcompete (overtake) our native flora, which in turn affects animals and birds that depend on them for food. Noxious weeds can be harmful to wildlife. Yes, just like birds and furry critters, we humans can carry weed seeds from one place to another. Here are a couple of things hikers can do to minimize the spread of noxious weeds. First, learn to identify noxious weeds and exotic species. You can obtain a provincial field guide from the B.C. Ministry of Agriculture, Fisheries, and Food (www.agf. gov.bc.ca/cropprot/weedguid/weedguid.htm). Second, regularly clean your boots, tents, packs, and hiking poles of mud and seeds. Brush your dog to remove any weed seeds. Avoid camping and traveling in weed-infested areas.

• *Stay on the trail.* It's true, a path anywhere leads nowhere new, but purists will just have to get over it. Paths serve an important purpose: They limit our impact on natural areas. Straying from a designated trail may seem innocent, but it can cause damage to sensitive areas—damage that a wild spot may take years to recover from, if it can recover at all. Even simple shortcuts can be destructive. So, please, stay on the trail.

• *Keep your dog under control.* You can buy a flexi-lead that allows your dog to go exploring along the trail while allowing you the ability to reel her in should another hiker approach or should she decide to chase a deer or black bear. Always obey leash laws and be sure to bury your dog's waste or pack it out in resealable plastic bags. In many B.C. parks, dogs are prohibited in the backcountry.

• *Respect other trail users.* Often you're not the only one on the trail. With the rise in popularity of multiuse trails, you'll have to learn a new kind of respect, beyond the nod and "hello" approach you're used to. You should first investigate whether you're on a multiuse trail, and assume the appropriate precautions. When you encounter motorized vehicles (ATVs, motorcycles, and 4WDs), be acutely aware. Though they should *always* yield to the hiker, often they're going too fast or are too lost in the buzz of their engine to react to your presence. If you hear activity ahead, step off the trail just to be safe. You're not likely to hear mountain bikers coming, so the best bet is to know whether you share the trail with them. Cyclists should *always* yield to hikers, but that's of little comfort to the hiker. Be aware. When you approach horses or pack animals on the trail, always step quietly off the trail, preferably on the downhill side, and let them pass. If you're wearing a large backpack, it's often a good idea to sit down. To some animals, a hiker wearing a large backpack might appear threatening.

GETTING INTO SHAPE

Unless you want to be sore—and possibly have to shorten your trip or vacation —be sure to get in shape before a big hike. If you're terribly out of shape, start a walking program early, preferably eight weeks in advance. Start with a fifteen-minute walk during your lunch hour or after work and gradually increase your walking time to an hour. You should also increase your elevation gain. Walking briskly up hills really strengthens your leg muscles and gets your heart rate up. If you work in a storied office building, take the stairs instead of the elevator. If you prefer going to a gym, walk the treadmill or use a StairMaster. You can further increase your strength and endurance by walking with a loaded backpack. Stationary exercises you might consider are squats, leg lifts, sit-ups, and push-ups. Other good ways to get in shape include biking, running, aerobics, and, of course, short hikes.

PREPAREDNESS

It's been said that failing to plan means planning to fail. So do take the necessary time to plan your trip. Whether going on a short day hike or an extended backpack trip, always prepare for the worst. Simply remembering to pack a copy of the *Canadian Forces Survival Manual* is not preparedness. Although it's not a bad idea if you plan on entering truly wild places, it's merely the tourniquet answer to a problem. You need to do your best to prevent the problem from arising in the first place. These days the word *survival* is often replaced with the pathetically feeble term *comfort*. In order to remain comfortable (and to survive if you really want to push it), you need to concern yourself with the basics: water, food, and shelter. Don't go on a hike without having these bases covered. And don't go on a hike expecting to find these items in the woods.

Water

Even in frigid conditions, you need at least two liters of water a day to function efficiently. Add heat and/or taxing terrain and you can bump that figure up to four liters. That's simply a base to work from—your metabolism and your level of conditioning can raise or lower that amount. Unless you know your level, assume that you need four liters of water a day. Now, where do you plan on getting the water?

Natural water sources can be loaded with intestinal disturbers, such as bacteria and viruses. *Giardia lamblia*, the most common of these disturbers, is a protozoan parasite that lives part of its life cycle as a cyst in water sources. The parasite spreads when mammals (humans included) defecate in water sources. Once ingested, *Giardia* can induce cramping, diarrhea, vomiting, and fatigue within two days to two weeks. *Giardia* is treatable with prescription drugs. If you believe you've contracted *Giardia*, see a doctor immediately.

Treating Water

The best and easiest way to avoid polluted water is to carry your water with you. Yet depending on the nature of your hike and the duration, this may not be an option. In that case, you'll need to look into treating water. Regardless of which method you choose, you should always carry some water with you, in case of an emergency. Save this reserve until you absolutely need it.

There are three methods of treating water: boiling, chemical treatment, and filtering. Boiling is the safest (if not simplest) method because it's not dependent on variables such as brand name or proper dosage. If you boil water, it's recommended that you do so for ten to fifteen minutes, though some will say just bringing the water to a boil is enough. Many may find this method impractical, since you're forced to exhaust a good deal of your fuel supply. You can opt for chemical treatment (such as Potable Aqua), which will kill *Giardia* but will not take care of other chemical pollutants. Other drawbacks to chemical treatments are the unpleasant taste of the water after it's treated and the length of time it takes for them to be effective. You can remedy the former by adding powdered drink mix to the water. Filters are the preferred method for treating water. Filters (check the instructions to make sure) remove *Giardia*, organic and inorganic contaminants, and don't leave an aftertaste. Some filters also remove viruses. Water filters are far from perfect, as they can easily become clogged or leak if a gasket wears out. It's always a good idea to carry a backup supply of chemical treatment tablets in case your filter decides to quit on you.

Food

If we're talking about "survival," you can go days without food, as long as you have water. But we're talking about "comfort" here. Try to avoid foods that are high in sugar and fat such as candy bars and potato chips. These food types are harder to digest and are low in nutritional value. Instead, bring along foods that are easy to pack, nutritious, and high in energy (say, bagels, nutrition bars, dehydrated fruit, nut mixes, and jerky). Complex carbohydrates and protein are your best food friends. If you are on an overnight trip, easy-to-fix dinners include rice or pasta dinners and soup mixes. A few spices are lightweight and can really perk up a meal. Freeze-dried meals are nice for long trips, but are expensive and bulky. If you do a lot of long backpacks, invest in a dehydrator. For a tasty breakfast, you can fix hot oatmeal with brown sugar and reconstituted milk or soy powder topped off with banana chips. If you like a hot drink in the morning, bring along herbal tea bags or hot chocolate. If you are a coffee junkie, you can purchase coffee that is packaged like tea bags. Prepackage all your meals in heavy-duty resealable plastic bags to keep food from spilling in your pack. These bags can be reused to pack out trash. Prepackaging also minimizes extra trash in the form of boxes and cans. Avoid bringing glass containers into the backcountry—broken glass can pose some serious problems. A good book on backcountry cooking is *Wilderness Ranger Cookbook* by Brunell and Swain from Falcon Press, the proceeds of which go to training wilderness rangers. Another good book is *Simple Foods for the Pack*, published by the Sierra Club.

Shelter

The type of shelter you choose depends less on the conditions than on your tolerance for discomfort. Shelter comes in many forms—tent, tarp, lean to, bivy sack, cabin, cave, and so on. If you're camping in the desert, a bivy sack may suffice, but if you're near tree line and a storm is approaching, a better choice is a three- or four-season tent. Tents are the logical and most popular choice for most backpackers because they're lightweight and packable—and you can rest assured that you always have shelter from the elements. (There's more on tents later on in this section.) Before you leave on your trip, anticipate what the weather and terrain will be like and bring the type of shelter that will work best for your comfort level.

Finding a Campsite

If there are established campsites, stick to those. If not, start looking for a campsite early—around 3:30 or 4:00 P.M. Stop at the first appropriate site you see, remembering that good campsites are found and not made. Depending on the area, it could be a long time before you find another suitable location. Pitch your camp in an area that's reasonably level and clear of underbrush (which can harbor insects and conceal approaching animals). Make sure the area is at least 60 meters from fragile areas such as lakeshores, meadows, and stream banks. Woody-stemmed plants like kinnikinnick are easily damaged, so avoid plopping your tent on top of them. Try to avoid camping above the tree line, because the alpine is fragile, and you're exposing yourself to possible high winds and unexpected snowstorms.

If you are camping in stormy, rainy weather, look for a rock outcrop or a shelter in the trees to keep the wind from blowing your tent all night. Be sure that you don't camp under trees with dead limbs that might break off on top of you. Also, try to find an area that has an absorbent surface, such as sandy soil or forest duff. This, in addition to camping on a surface with a slight angle, will provide better drainage. By all means, don't dig trenches to provide drainage around your tent—remember, you're practicing minimum-impact camping.

Since most of Vancouver Island is bear country, steer clear of creekbeds and animal paths. If you see any signs of a bear's presence (such as scat or footprints), relocate. You'll need to find a campsite near a tall tree where you can hang your food and other items that may attract bears such as deodorant, toothpaste, or soap. Carry a lightweight nylon rope for this purpose. As a rule, you should hang your food at least 5 meters from the ground and 1½ meters away from the tree trunk. Trees at higher elevations don't often have branches longer than this, so you may need to string rope between two trees or find a leaning snag. You can put food and other items in a waterproof stuff sack and tie one end of the rope to the stuff sack. To get the other end of the rope over the tree branch, tie a good-sized rock to it and gently toss the rock over the tree branch. Pull the stuff sack up until it reaches the top of the branch and tie it off securely. Don't hang your food near your tent! If possible, hang your food at least 35 meters away from your campsite. Alternatives to hanging your food are bearproof plastic tubes and metal bear boxes. Many B.C. Parks now provide bearproof food caches. Squirrels, mice, and whiskey jacks will also steal your food if given the opportunity.

Lastly, think of comfort. Lie down on the ground where you intend to sleep and see if it's a good fit. Bring along an insulating pad for warmth and extra comfort. The days of using pine boughs or digging a hip depression in the ground are long gone. And for the final touch, have your tent face east. You'll appreciate the warmth of the morning sun and have a nice view to wake up to.

FIRST AID

If you plan to spend a lot of time outdoors hiking, spend a few hours and bucks to take a good wilderness or mountain-oriented first-aid class. You'll learn not only first-aid basics but also how to be creative miles from nowhere. See the appendix for a list of clubs and organizations that can help put you in touch with training options.

Now, we know you're tough, but get 20 kilometers into the woods and develop a blister, and you'll wish you had carried a first-aid kit. Face it: It's just plain good sense. Many companies produce lightweight, compact first-aid kits; just make sure yours contains at least the following:

First Aid

- Band-Aids
- moleskin, duct tape, or athletic tape
- various sterile gauze and dressings
- white surgical tape
- an Ace bandage
- an antihistamine
- aspirin, ibuprofen, or acetaminophen

- a first-aid book
- antacids
- tweezers
- scissors
- antibacterial wipes
- triple antibiotic ointment
- plastic gloves
- sterile cotton-tip applicators
- a thermometer

Here are a few tips for dealing with and hopefully preventing certain ailments.

Sunburn

To avoid sunburn, wear sunscreen (SPF 15 or higher), protective clothing, and a wide-brimmed hat when you are hiking in sunny weather. If you do get sunburned, treat the area with aloe vera gel and protect the area from further sun exposure. Protect your eyes by wearing sunglasses with UV protection, too!

Blisters

First, try to prevent blisters. Break in your boots, wear appropriate socks, and then, if you're prone to blisters, apply moleskin, duct tape, or athletic tape *before* you start hiking to help decrease friction to that area. In case a blister develops despite your careful precautions, an effective way to treat it is to cut out a circle of moleskin and remove the center—like a doughnut—and place it over the blistered area. Cutting out the center will reduce the pressure applied to sensitive skin. Then put moleskin in the hole and tape over the whole mess. A thin coating of tincture of Benzoin will help keep your moleskin in place.

Insect Bites and Stings

The most troublesome of Vancouver Island's insects are mosquitoes, wasps, and ticks. A simple treatment for most insect bites and stings is to apply hydrocortisone 1 percent cream topically and to take a pain medication such as ibuprofen or acetaminophen to reduce swelling. If you forgot to pack these items, a cold compress or a paste of mud and ashes can sometimes assuage the itching and discomfort. Remove any stingers by using tweezers or scraping the area with your fingernail or a knife blade. Don't pinch the area; you'll only spread the venom.

Some hikers are highly sensitive to bites and stings and may have a serious allergic reaction that can be life threatening. Symptoms of a serious allergic reaction can include wheezing, an asthmatic attack, and shock. The treatment for this severe type of reaction is epinephrine (adrenaline). If you know that you are sensitive to bites and stings, carry a prepackaged kit of epinephrine (such as Anakit or Epipen), which can be obtained from your local pharmacy. Also carry an antihistamine such as Benadryl.

Ticks

On Vancouver Island the western black-legged tick *(Ixodes pacificus)* is common during spring and early summer. The red and black females and smaller males attach to humans, deer, and domestic pets, engorging as they feed. While the tick is a carrier of the microorganism responsible for Lyme disease in the United States, the same microorganism is less common in Canada and has not yet been detected on Vancouver Island. The best defense is, of course, prevention. If you know you're going to be hiking through an area littered with ticks, wear long pants and a long-sleeved shirt. At the end of your hike, do a spot check for ticks (and insects in general). If you do find a tick, coat the insect with Vaseline or tree sap to cut off its air supply. The tick should release its hold, but if it doesn't, grab the head of the tick firmly—with a pair of tweezers if you have them—and gently pull it away from the skin with a twisting motion. Sometimes the mouthparts linger, embedded in your skin. If this happens, try to remove them with a disinfected needle. Clean the affected area with an antibacterial cleanser and then apply triple antibiotic ointment. Monitor the area for a few days. If irritation persists or a white spot develops, see a doctor for possible infection.

Stinging Nettle

This skin irritant *(Urtica diocia)* can be found in meadows, thickets, stream banks, and open forests across Vancouver Island. It often grows in disturbed habitats and always finds a home in moist soil. Learn how to spot the dense drooping clusters of spikes hanging beneath serrated leaves. The formic acid secreted by the plant causes an irritating skin reaction immediately after contact. The painful, itchy rash can last for several days. The best defense against stinging nettle is to wear protective clothing. If you've been exposed, wash the area as soon as possible with soap and cool water. Taking a hot shower after you return home from your hike will also help to remove any lingering oil from your skin.

Snakebites

First off, there are no poisonous snakes on Vancouver Island. Second, snakebites are extremely rare. Unless startled or provoked, the majority of snakes will not bite. If you are wise to their habitats and keep a careful eye on the trail, you should be just fine. Though your chances of being struck are slim, it's wise to know what to do in the event you are.

If a *nonpoisonous* snake bites you, allow the wound to bleed a small amount and then cleanse the wounded area with a solution of 10 percent povidone iodine. Rinse the wound with clean water (preferably) or fresh urine (it might sound ugly, but it's sterile). Once the area is clean, cover it with triple antibiotic ointment and a clean bandage. Remember, most residual damage from snakebites, poisonous or otherwise, comes from infection, not the snake's venom. Keep the area as clean as possible and get medical attention immediately.

Dehydration

Have you ever hiked in hot weather and had a roaring headache and felt fatigued after only a few kilometers? More than likely you were dehydrated. Symptoms of dehydration include fatigue, headache, and decreased coordination and judgment. Dehydration can also make you more susceptible to hypothermia and frostbite. When you are hiking, your body's rate of fluid loss depends on the outside temperature, humidity, altitude, and your activity level. On average, a hiker walking in warm weather will lose four liters of fluid a day. That fluid loss is easily replaced by normal consumption of liquids and food. However, if you are walking briskly in hot, dry weather and hauling a heavy pack, you can lose one to three liters of water an hour. It's important to always carry plenty of water and to stop often and drink fluids regularly, even if you aren't thirsty. One way to tell if you're adequately hydrated is to check the color of your urine. It should be clear. The darker yellow it is, the more dehydrated you are. With a little creativity, you can check the color in the backcountry. You can also pinch the skin on the back of your hand. If it quickly lowers itself, you're okay; if it remains in a peak, you're dehydrated.

Heat Exhaustion

Heat exhaustion is the result of a loss of large amounts of electrolytes and often occurs if a hiker is dehydrated and has been under heavy exertion. Common symptoms of heat exhaustion include cramping, exhaustion, fatigue, lightheadedness, and nausea. You can treat heat exhaustion by getting out of the sun, eating high-energy foods, and drinking an electrolyte solution made up of one teaspoon of salt and one tablespoon of sugar dissolved in a liter of water. Drink this solution slowly over a period of one hour. Drinking plenty of fluids can also prevent heat exhaustion. When drinking a lot of water, remember to snack while you drink. If you don't, you'll disrupt the electrolyte balance as you lose body salt through sweating, and possibly develop hyponatremia (water intoxication). Symptoms include nausea, vomiting, frequent urination, and altered mental states. Avoid hiking during the hottest parts of the day and wear breathable clothing, a wide-brimmed hat, and sunglasses.

Hypothermia

Hypothermia is one of the biggest dangers in the backcountry—especially for day hikers in summertime. That may sound strange, but imagine starting out on a hike in midsummer when it's sunny and 25 degrees C out. You're clad in nylon shorts and a cotton T-shirt. About halfway through your hike, the sky begins to cloud up; in the next hour a light drizzle or snow begins to fall, and the wind starts to pick up. Before you know it, you are soaking wet and shivering—the perfect recipe for hypothermia. More advanced signs include decreased coordination, slurred speech, and blurred vision. When a victim's temperature falls below 32.8 degrees C, the blood pressure, breathing, and pulse plummet, possibly leading to coma and death.

To avoid hypothermia, always bring a windproof and rainproof shell, a fleece jacket, quick-drying tights or rain pants, gloves, and hat when you are hiking in the mountains. Avoid wearing 100 percent cotton clothing, because it does not dry easily and provides no warmth when wet. Learn to adjust your clothing layers based on the temperature. If you are climbing uphill at a moderate pace you will stay warm, but when you stop for a break you'll become cold quickly, unless you add more layers of clothing. Keeping hydrated and well nourished are also important in avoiding hypothermia.

If a hiker is showing advanced signs of hypothermia, dress her in dry clothes and make sure she is wearing a hat and gloves. Place her in a sleeping bag in a tent or shelter that will protect her from the wind and other elements. Give her warm fluids to drink and keep her awake. Put water bottles filled with warm water in the crotch and armpits to help warm her.

Frostbite

When the mercury dips below 0 degrees C, your extremities begin to chill. If a persistent chill attacks a localized area, say your hands or your toes, the circulatory system reacts by cutting off blood flow to the affected area—the idea being to protect and preserve the body's overall temperature. And so it's death by attrition for the affected area. Ice crystals start to form from the water in the cells of the neglected tissue. Deprived of heat, nourishment, and now water, the tissue literally starves. This is frostbite.

Prevention is your best defense against this situation. Most prone to frostbite are your face, hands, and feet—so protect these areas well. Wool is the material of choice because it provides ample air space for insulation and draws moisture away from the skin. However, synthetic fabrics have recently made great strides in the cold-weather clothing market. Do your research. A pair of light silk or polypro liners under your regular gloves or mittens is a good trick to keeping warm. They afford some additional warmth, but more importantly they'll allow you to remove your mitts for tedious work without exposing the skin.

Now, if your feet or hands start to feel cold or numb due to the elements, warm them as quickly as possible. Place cold hands under your armpits or bury them in your crotch. Carry hand and foot warmers if you can. If your feet are cold, change your socks. If there's plenty of room in your boots, add another pair of socks. Do remember, though, that constricting your feet in tight boots can restrict blood flow and actually make your feet colder more quickly. Your socks need to have breathing room if they're going to be effective. Dead air provides insulation. If your face is cold, place your warm hands over your face or simply wear a head stocking (called a balaclava).

Should your skin go numb and start to appear white and waxy but is still cold and soft, chances are you've got superficial frostbite. Rewarm as quickly as possible with skin-to-skin contact. No damage should occur. Do *not* let the area get frostbitten again!

If your skin is white and waxy but dents when you press on it, you have partial-thickness frostbite. Rewarm as you would for superficial frostbite, but expect swelling and blisters to form. Don't massage the affected area, but do take ibuprofen for pain and reduction of tissue damage. If blisters form, you need to leave the backcountry.

If your skin is frozen hard like an ice cube, you have full-thickness frostbite. Don't try to thaw the area unless you can maintain the warmth. In other words, don't stop to warm up your frostbitten feet only to head back on the trail. You'll do more damage than good. Tests have shown that hikers who walked on thawed feet did more harm, and endured more pain, than hikers who left the affected areas alone. Do your best to get out of the cold entirely and seek medical attention—which usually consists of performing a rapid rewarming in warm water (40 to 42 degrees C) for twenty to thirty minutes. Get to a doctor as soon as possible!

The overall objective in preventing both hypothermia and frostbite is to keep the body's core warm. Protect key areas where heat escapes, like the top of the head, and maintain the proper nutrition and hydration levels. Foods that are high in calories aid the body in producing heat. Never smoke or drink alcohol when you're in situations where the cold is threatening. By affecting blood flow, these activities ultimately cool the body's core temperature.

Hantavirus Pulmonary Syndrome (HPS)

While cases of HPS on the B.C. coast are extremely rare, they have happened. Deer mice spread the virus that causes HPS, and humans contract it from breathing it in, usually when they've disturbed an area with dust and mice feces from nests or surfaces with mice droppings or urine. Exposure to large numbers of rodents and their feces or urine presents the greatest risk. As hikers, we sometimes enter old buildings, and often deer mice live in these places. We may not be around long enough to be exposed, but do be aware of this disease. About half the people who develop HPS die. Symptoms are flu-like and appear about two to three weeks after exposure. After initial symptoms, a dry cough and shortness of breath follow. Breathing is difficult. If you even think you might have HPS, see a doctor immediately!

NATURAL HAZARDS

Besides tripping over a rock or tree root on the trail, there are some real hazards to be aware of while hiking. Vancouver Island doesn't have the plethora of poisonous snakes and plants, insects, and grizzly bears found in other parts of Canada, but there are a few weather conditions and predators to take into account.

• *Flash floods.* Flash floods on Vancouver Island usually come in the form of a swollen stream or river. Overnight rainstorms, particularly the voluminous sort received by the Island's west coast, may change a babbling brook into a roaring river in less than six hours. When traveling in areas prone to heavy precipitation, take extra food and clothing and be prepared to sit tight. Flash floods usually subside quickly, so be patient and don't cross a swollen stream.

• *Bears.* Though Vancouver Island has no grizzly bears, black bears are plentiful. Sightings tend to increase the farther north you travel. Here are some tips in case you and a bear scare each other. Most of all, avoid scaring a bear. Watch for bear tracks (five toes) and droppings (sizable with leaves, partly digested berries, seeds, and/or animal fur). Talk or sing where visibility or hearing is limited. Keep a clean camp, hang food, and don't sleep in the clothes you wore while cooking. Be especially careful in spring to avoid getting between a mother and her cubs. In late summer and fall, bears are busy eating berries and fish to fatten up for winter, so be extra careful around berry bushes and spawning streams. If you do encounter a bear, move away slowly while facing the bear, talk softly, and avoid direct eye contact. Give the bear room to escape. Never approach wildlife to get that "good shot." Believe it or not, we've seen individuals advance on bears to capture them on film, an act of ignorance that more often than not results in a dead bear. Bears have the same right to be left alone that you do. Give them their space. If a bear stands upright to get a better whiff of you, or decides to charge you to try to intimidate you, try to stay calm. If a bear does attack you, fight back with anything you have handy. Unleashed dogs have been known to come running back to their owners with a bear close behind. Keep your dog on a leash or leave her at home.

• *Cougars.* Cougars appear to be getting more comfortable around humans as long as deer (their favorite prey) are in an area with adequate cover. Usually elusive and quiet, cougars rarely attack people, yet British Columbia has seen several attacks in recent years. If you meet a cougar, give the animal a chance to escape. Stay calm and talk firmly. Back away slowly while facing the cougar. If you run, you'll only encourage the curious cat to chase you. Make yourself look large by opening a jacket, if you have one, or waving your hiking poles. If the cougar behaves aggressively, throw stones, sticks, or whatever you can while remaining tall. If a cougar does attack, fight for your life with anything you can grab.

NAVIGATION

Whether you are going on a short hike in a familiar area or planning a week-long backpack trip, you should always be equipped with the proper navigational equipment—at the very least a detailed map and a sturdy compass. These tools are only useful if you know how to use them. Courses and books are available, so make sure your skills are up to snuff.

Maps

There are many different types of maps available to help you find your way on the trail. Easiest to find are forest service maps and provincial park maps. These maps tend to cover large areas, so be sure they are detailed enough for your particular trip. You can also obtain national park maps as well as high-quality maps from private companies and trail groups. These maps can be obtained from either outdoor stores or tourism info centers. Being large, these maps are best used for trip planning and driving, but not to navigate in the backcountry. Canadian Hydrographic Service national topographic systems (NTS) maps (topos) are particularly popular with hikers—especially serious backcountry hikers. These maps contain the standard map symbols such as roads, lakes, and rivers, as well as contour lines that show the details of the trail terrain like ridges, valleys, passes, and mountain peaks. To purchase topo maps, contact the Center for Topographic Information, Natural Resources Canada, 615 Booth Street, Room 711, Ottawa, Ontario K1A 0E9; phone (800) 465–6277; Web site at maps.nrcan.gc.ca/topographic.html.

The art of map reading is a skill that you can develop by first practicing in an area you are familiar with. To begin, orient the map so it's lined up in the correct direction (north on the map is lined up with true north). Next, familiarize yourself with the map symbols and try and match them up with terrain features around you such as a high ridge, mountain peak, river, or lake. If you are practicing with an NTS map, notice the contour lines. On gentler terrain these contour lines are spaced farther apart, and on steeper terrain they are closer together. Pick a short loop trail and stop frequently to check your position on the map. As you practice map reading, you'll learn how to anticipate a steep section on the trail, or a good place to take a rest break, or the like.

A couple of good books on orienteering are June Fleming's *Staying Found* and *Using a Map and Compass* by Don Geary.

Compasses

First off, the sun is not a substitute for a compass. So what kind of compass should you have? Here are some characteristics you should look for: a rectangular base with detailed scales, a liquid-filled housing, protective housing, a sighting line on the mirror, luminous alignment and back-bearing arrows, a luminous north-seeking arrow, and a well-defined bezel ring.

courtesy Johnson Outdoors

You can learn compass basics by reading the detailed instructions included with your compass. If you want to fine-tune your compass skills, sign up for an orienteering class or purchase a book on compass reading. Once you've learned the basic skills on using a compass, remember to practice these skills before you head into the backcountry.

Because magnetic north keeps moving around the North Pole and topo maps use true north, using a map and compass together requires making adjustments for declination (the difference between magnetic and true north). Topo maps show the declination, but if you are looking at a 1970 map, the declination has changed since then.

Global Positioning Systems (GPS)

If you are a klutz at using a compass, you may be interested in checking out the technical wizardry of the GPS device. The GPS was developed by the U.S. Pentagon and works off twenty-four NAVSTAR satellites, which were designed to guide missiles to their targets. A GPS device is a handheld unit that calculates your latitude and longitude with the easy press of a button. The U.S. Department of Defense used to scramble the satellite signals a bit to prevent civilians (and spies!) from getting extremely accurate readings, but that practice was discontinued in May 2000, and GPS units now provide nearly pinpoint accuracy—to within 10 to 20 meters.

There are many different types of GPS units available, and they range in price from $100 to $400. In general, all GPS units have a display screen and keypad where you input information. In addition to acting as a compass, the unit allows you to plot your route, retrace your path, track your traveling speed, find the mileage between waypoints (straight-line distance), and calculate the total mileage of your route. Despite the advances in GPS technology, don't put all of your trust in your GPS. Keep in mind that these devices don't pick up signals indoors, in heavily wooded areas, or in deep valleys. And most important to remember, they run on batteries.

Pedometers

A pedometer is a handy device that can track your mileage as you hike. This device is a small, clip-on unit with a digital display that calculates your hiking distance in miles or kilometers based on your walking stride. Some units also calculate the calories you burn and your total hiking time. Pedometers are available at most large outdoor stores and range in price from $20 to $40.

TRIP PLANNING

Planning your hiking adventure begins with letting a friend or relative know your trip itinerary so they can call for help if you don't return at your scheduled time. Your next task is to make sure you are outfitted to experience the risks and rewards of the trail. This section highlights gear and clothing you may want to take with you to get the most out of your hike.

EQUIPMENT

With the outdoor market currently flooded with products, many of which are pure gimmickry, it seems impossible to both differentiate and choose. Do I really need a tropical-fish-lined collapsible shower? (No, you don't.) The only defense against the maddening quantity of items thrust in your face is to think practically—and to do so before you go shopping. The worst buys are impulsive buys. Since most of your name brands will differ only slightly in quality, it's best to know what you're looking for in terms of function. Buy only what you need. You will, don't forget, be carrying what you've bought on your back. Here are some things to keep in mind before you go shopping. Your pack should weigh no more than 30 percent of your body weight.

Clothes

Clothing is your armor against Mother Nature's little surprises. Vancouver Island's weather can range from blistering heat to brutal cold, and hikers should be prepared for any possibility, especially when hiking in mountainous areas. Expect snow any month of the year and afternoon showers. The sun may feel

Day Hike

- day pack
- water and water bottles/ water hydration system
- food and high-energy snacks
- first-aid kit
- headlamp/flashlight with extra batteries and bulbs
- maps and compass/ GPS unit
- knife/multipurpose tool
- sunscreen and sunglasses
- matches in waterproof container and fire starter
- insulating top and bottom layers (fleece, wool, etc.)
- rain gear
- winter hat and gloves
- wide-brimmed sun hat
- bear spray/bear bangers
- insect repellent
- backpacker's trowel, toilet paper, and resealable plastic bags
- whistle and/or mirror
- space blanket/bag
- camera/film
- guidebook
- watch
- water treatment tablets
- Wet Ones or other wet wipes
- hand and foot warmers if hiking high
- duct tape for repairs
- extra socks
- gaiters depending on season
- sanitary products

hot until a cloud comes along, and instantly the air temperature feels very cool. With the changeable weather and cool temperatures at high altitudes, adequate rain protection and layered clothes are good ideas.

During the summer, your main consideration is protecting your skin from sunburn and having layers to adapt to changeable weather conditions. Wearing long pants and a long-sleeved shirt made out of materials such as nylon will protect your skin from the damaging rays of the sun. Avoid wearing 100 percent cotton, which doesn't dry easily and offers no warmth when wet.

Since the weather can change from warm to chilly very quickly, if you wear a T-shirt and shorts, make sure you have top and bottom "insulating" layers (see below) in your pack. Aside from keeping you warm, this layer needs to "breathe" so you stay dry while hiking. A fabric that provides insulation and dries quickly is fleece. It's interesting to note that this one-of-a-kind fabric is made out of recycled plastic. Purchasing a zip-up jacket or pullover made of this material is highly recommended.

Overnight Trip

Everything listed for a
Day Hike, plus:

- backpack and waterproof
  rain cover
- bandanna
- biodegradable soap
- collapsible water container
  (1- to 2-liter capacity)
- clothing—extra wool socks,
  shirt and shorts, long pants
- cook set/utensils and pot
  scrubber
- stuff sacks to store gear
- extra plastic resealable bags
- garbage bags
- journal/pen

- nylon rope to hang food
- long underwear
- permit (if required)
- repair kit (tent, stove, pack,
  etc.)
- sandals or running shoes to
  wear around camp and to
  ford streams
- sleeping bag
- waterproof stuff sacks (one
  for hanging food)
- insulating ground pad
- hand towel
- stove and fuel
- tent and ground cloth
- toiletry items
- water filter

Another important layer is the "shell" layer. You'll need some type of waterproof, windproof, breathable jacket that'll fit over all of your other layers. It should have a large hood that fits over a hat. You'll also need a good pair of rain pants made from a similar waterproof, breathable fabric. A fabric that easily fits the bill is Gore-Tex. However, while a quality Gore-Tex jacket can range in price from $100 to $450, you should know that there are more affordable fabrics out there that work just as well.

Now that you've learned the basics of layering, you can't forget to protect your hands and face. In cold, windy, rainy, or snowy weather, you'll need a hat made of wool or fleece and insulated, waterproof gloves that will keep your hands warm and toasty. Buying a pair of light silk or polypro liners to wear under your regular gloves or mittens is a good idea. They'll allow you to remove your outer gloves for tedious work without exposing the skin. Even in summer, a light winter hat and gloves can really help, too. Remember that more than 50 percent of your body heat is lost through your head, so if your extremities are cold, put on that hat! Carry packages of hand and foot warmers if you plan to be above tree line in case it gets really cold or snowy.

For winter hiking or snowshoeing, you'll need yet a lower "wicking" layer of long underwear that keeps perspiration away from your skin. Wearing long underwear made from synthetic fibers such as Capilene, Coolmax, or Thermax is an excellent choice. These fabrics wick moisture away from the skin and draw it toward the next layer of clothing, where it then evaporates. Avoid wearing long underwear made of cotton as it is slow to dry and keeps moisture next to your skin.

Footwear

If you have any extra money to spend on your trip, put that money into boots or trail shoes. Poor-fitting boots will bring a hike to a halt faster than anything else. To avoid this annoyance, buy boots that provide support and are lightweight and flexible. When you purchase footwear, go to an outdoor store that specializes in backpacking and camping equipment. Knowledgeable salespeople can really help you find the right boot and the right fit for the type of hiking/backpacking you want to do. A lightweight hiking boot that can be waterproofed is usually adequate for most day hikes and short backpacks. Trail running shoes provide a little extra cushion and are made in a high-top style that many people wear for hiking. These running shoes are lighter, more flexible, and more breathable than hiking boots. Sturdier boots may be your best bet for rugged trails and multiday backpacks. If you know you'll be hiking in wet weather or crossing streams or muddy areas often, purchase boots or shoes with a Gore-Tex liner, which will help keep your feet dry. Especially during spring and early summer when trails are muddy or snowy, make sure you wear waterproofed boots for maximum dryness. Walking around mud holes and snow damages wet ground and makes a bigger muddy mess. Get muddy! It's easier to clean your boots than repair damaged vegetation.

When buying your boots, be sure to wear the same type of socks you'll be wearing on the trail. If the boots you're buying are for heavy-duty or cold-weather hiking, try the boots on while wearing two pairs of socks. Speaking of socks, a good sock combination is to wear a thinner sock made of wool or polypro/nylon covered by a heavier outer sock made of wool or wool/acrylic blend. The inner sock protects the foot from the rubbing effects of the outer sock and prevents blisters. Many outdoor stores have some type of ramp to simulate hiking uphill and downhill. Be sure to take advantage of this test; toe-jamming boot fronts can be very painful and debilitating on the downhill trek.

Once you've purchased your footwear, be sure to break them in before you hit the trail. New footwear is often stiff and needs to be stretched and molded to your foot. A little leather conditioner can help the break-in process without major destruction to your foot in the process.

Hiking Poles

Hiking with poles brings interesting comments ranging from "There's no snow now" to "Wow! I wish I had a pair of those on this trail!" Hiking poles help with balance and, more importantly, take pressure off your knees. The ones with shock absorbers are easier on your elbows and your knees. Some poles even come with a camera attachment to be used as a monopod. And should you—heaven forbid—meet a cougar, bear, or unfriendly dog, those poles make you look a lot bigger.

Packs

No matter what type of hiking you do, you'll need a pack of some sort to carry the basic trail essentials. There are a variety of backpacks on the market, but let's first discuss what you intend to use it for. Day hikes or overnight trips?

If you plan on doing a day hike, a daypack should have some of the following characteristics: a padded hip belt that's at least 5 centimeters in diameter (avoid packs with only a small nylon piece of webbing for a hip belt); a chest strap (the chest strap helps stabilize the pack against your body); external pockets to carry water and other items that you want easy access to; an internal pocket to hold keys, a knife, a wallet, and other miscellaneous items; an external lashing system to hold a jacket; and maybe a hydration pocket for carrying a hydration system (which consists of a water bladder with an attachable drinking hose).

For short hikes, some hikers like to use a fanny pack to store just a camera, food, a compass, a map, and other trail essentials. Most fanny packs have pockets for two water bottles and a padded hip belt.

If you intend to do an extended, overnight trip, there are multiple considerations. First off, you need to decide what kind of framed pack you want. There are two backpack types for backpacking: the internal frame and the external frame. An internal-frame pack rests closer to your body, making it more stable and easier to balance when hiking over rough terrain. An external-frame pack is just that, an aluminum frame attached to the exterior of the pack. An external frame pack is better for long backpack trips because it distributes the pack weight better, and you can carry heavier loads. It's easier to pack, and your gear is more accessible. It also offers better back ventilation in hot weather.

courtesy Johnson Coleman

The most critical measurement for fitting a pack is torso length. The pack needs to rest evenly on your hips without sagging. A good pack will come in two or three sizes and have straps and hip belts that are adjustable according to your body size and characteristics.

When you purchase a backpack, go to an outdoor store with salespeople who are knowledgeable in how to properly fit a pack. Once the pack is fitted for you, load it with the amount of weight you plan on taking on the trail. The weight of the pack should be distributed evenly and you should be able to swing your arms and walk briskly without feeling out of balance. Another good technique for evaluating a pack is to walk up and down stairs and make quick turns to the right and to the left to be sure the pack doesn't feel out of balance.

Other features that are nice to have on a backpack include a removable day pack or fanny pack, external pockets for extra water, and extra lash points to attach a jacket or other items. Remember all these extra features add weight to the basic pack, cutting down on the amount of other stuff you can carry.

Sleeping Bags and Pads

Sleeping bags are rated by temperature. You can purchase a bag made of synthetic fiber, or you can buy a goose down bag. Goose down bags are more expensive, but they have a higher insulating capacity by weight and will keep their loft longer. You'll want to purchase a bag with a temperature rating that fits the time of year and conditions you are most likely to camp in. One caveat: The techno-standard for temperature ratings is far from perfect. Ratings vary from manufacturer to manufacturer, so to protect yourself you should purchase a bag rated 6 to 8 degrees C below the temperature you expect to be camping in. Synthetic bags are more resistant to water than down bags, but many down bags are now made with a Gore-Tex shell that helps to repel water. Down bags are also more compressible than synthetic bags and take up less room in your pack, which is an important consideration if you are planning a multiday backpack trip. Make sure to buy a compression stuff sack for your sleeping bag to minimize the space it consumes in your backpack. Features to look for in a sleeping bag include: a mummy-style bag, a hood you can cinch down around your head in cold weather, and draft tubes along the zippers that help keep heat in and drafts out.

You'll also want a sleeping pad to provide insulation and padding from the cold ground. There are different types of sleeping pads available, from the more expensive self-inflating air mattresses like Therm-a-Rest to the less expensive closed-cell foam pads such as Ridge Rest. Self-inflating air mattresses are usually heavier than closed-cell foam mattresses and prone to punctures but can be repaired.

Tents

The tent is your home away from home while on the trail. It provides protection from wind, snow, rain, and insects. A three-season tent is a good choice for backpacking and can range in price from $100 to $600. These lightweight and versatile tents provide protection in all types of weather, except heavy snow-

storms or high winds, and range in weight from one and a half to three kilograms. Look for a tent that's easy to set up and will easily fit two people with gear. Dome-type tents usually offer more headroom and places to store gear. Other tent designs include a vestibule where you can store wet boots. Some nice-to-have items in a tent include interior pockets to store small items and lashing points to hang a clothesline. Most three-season tents also come with stakes so you can secure the tent in high winds. Before you purchase a tent, set it up and take it down a few times to be sure it is easy to handle. Also, sit inside the tent and make sure it has enough room for you and your gear.

Cell Phones

Many hikers are carrying their cell phones into the backcountry these days in case of emergency. That's fine and good, but please know that cell phone coverage is often poor to nonexistent in valleys, canyons, and thick forest. More importantly, people have started to call for help because they're tired or lost. Let's go back to being prepared. You are responsible for yourself in the backcountry. Use your brain to avoid problems, and if you do encounter one, first use your brain to try to correct the situation. Only use your cell phone—if it works—in cases of true emergencies.

HIKING WITH CHILDREN

Hiking with children isn't a matter of how many kilometers you can cover or how much elevation gain you make in a day, it's about seeing and experiencing nature through their eyes.

Kids like to explore and have fun. They like to stop and point out bugs and plants, look under rocks, jump in puddles, and throw sticks. If you're taking a toddler or young child on a hike, start with a trail that you're familiar with. Trails that have interesting things for kids, like piles of leaves to play in or a small stream to wade through during the summer, will make the hike much more enjoyable for them and will keep them from getting bored.

You can keep your child's attention if you have a strategy before starting on the trail. Using games is not only an effective way to keep a child's attention, it's also a great way to teach him or her about nature. Play hide and seek, where your child is the mouse and you are the hawk. Quiz children on the names of plants and animals. If your children are old enough, let them carry their own day packs filled with snacks and water. So that you are sure to go at their pace and not yours, let them lead the way. Playing follow the leader works particularly well when you have a group of children. Have each child take a turn at being the leader. *Sharing Nature with Children* by Joseph Cornell, Dawn Publications, describes excellent activities such as those above.

With children, a lot of clothing is key. You always want to bring extra clothing for your children no matter what the season. In winter have your children wear wool socks and warm layers such as long underwear, a Polarfleece jacket and hat, wool mittens, and good rain gear. It's not a bad idea to have these along in late fall and early spring as well. Good footwear is also important. A sturdy pair of high-top tennis shoes or lightweight hiking boots is the best bet for little ones. If you're hiking in the summer near a lake or stream, bring along old sneakers that your children can put on when they want to go exploring in the water. Remember when you're near any type of water, always watch children at all times. Also, keep a close eye on teething toddlers who may decide a rock or a poison mushroom is an interesting item to put in their mouth.

From spring through fall, you'll want your kids to wear a wide-brimmed hat to keep their face, head, and ears protected from the hot sun. Also, make sure your children wear sunscreen at all times. Choose a brand without PABA—

courtesy Johnson Outdoors

children have sensitive skin and may have an allergic reaction to sunscreen that contains PABA. If you are hiking with a child younger than six months, don't use sunscreen or insect repellent. Instead, be sure that the head, face, neck, and ears are protected from the sun with a wide-brimmed hat, and that all other skin exposed to the sun is protected with the appropriate clothing.

Remember that food is fun. Kids like snacks, so it's important to bring a lot of munchies for the trail. Stopping often for snack breaks is a fun way to keep the trail interesting. Raisins, apples, granola bars, crackers and cheese, cereal, and trail mix all make great snacks. If your children are old enough to carry their own backpack, fill it with treats before you leave. If your kids don't like drinking water, you can bring boxes of fruit juice.

Avoid poorly designed child-carrying packs—you don't want to break your back carrying your child. Most child-carrying backpacks designed to hold a fifteen-kilogram child will contain a large carrying pocket to hold diapers and other items. Some have an optional rain and sun hood. Mountain Equipment Co-op offers a number of specialized products for carrying children in addition to other outdoor gear for children.

Appendix

HIKES INDEX

To help you select a hike, we've categorized some of our favorite hikes by area of interest.

Best Hikes for Backpackers

Hike 20: Della Falls

Hike 26: Crest Mountain

Hike 27: Elk River Trail/Landslide Lake

Hike 28: Marble Meadows

Hike 30: Bedwell Lake

Hike 31: Schoen Lake

Hike 33: San Josef Bay/Mount St. Patrick

Hike 34: Cape Scott

Hike 36: Juan de Fuca Marine Trail

Hike 38: West Coast Trail

Hike 39: Carmanah Valley

Hike 40: Walbran Valley

Hike 41: Clayoquot Valley Witness Trail

Hike 50: Nootka Island

Best Hikes for Coastal and Marine Life

Hike 2: Roche Cove Regional Park

Hike 3: East Sooke Regional Park

Hike 8: Maple Mountain

Hike 9: Cable Bay Nature Trail and Dodd Narrows

Hike 12: Newcastle Island Provincial Marine Park

Hike 32: Raft Cove

Hike 33: San Josef Bay/Mount St. Patrick

Hike 34: Cape Scott

Hike 35: Beautiful Bay

Hike 36: Juan de Fuca Marine Trail

Hike 37: Botanical Beach Provincial Park

Hike 38: West Coast Trail

Hike 42: Wild Pacific Trail

Hike 43: Gold Mine Trail

Hike 44: South Beach Trail

Hike 45: Wickaninnish Trail

Hike 48: Spruce Fringe

Hike 49: Schooner Trail

Hike 50: Nootka Island

Best Hikes for Children and Beginning Hikers

Hike 2: Roche Cove Regional Park

Hike 4: Thetis Lake

Hike 6: Cowichan River Footpath

Hike 8: Maple Mountain

Hike 9: Cable Bay Nature Trail and Dodd Narrows

Hike 10: Piper's Lagoon Park

Hike 11: Morrell Nature Sanctuary

Hike 12: Newcastle Island Provincial Marine Park

Hike 13: Notch Hill

Hike 15: Englishman River/Morrison Creek

Hike 16: Little Qualicum Falls Provincial Park

Hike 17: Cathedral Grove–MacMillan Provincial Park

Hike 22: Puntledge River Trail

Hike 25: Elk Falls Provincial Park

Hike 29: Upper Myra Falls

Hike 33: San Josef Bay/Mount St. Patrick

Hike 35: Beautiful Bay

Hike 43: Gold Mine Trail

Hike 44: South Beach Trail

Hike 45: Wickaninnish Trail

Hike 46: Shorepine Bog

Hike 47: Rainforest Figure Eight

Hike 48: Spruce Fringe

Hike 49: Schooner Trail

Best Hikes for Alpine and Subalpine Landscapes

Hike 18: Mount Arrowsmith (Ridge Access Routes)

Hike 20: Della Falls

Hike 21: Alone Mountain

Hike 23: Boston Ridge/Mount Becher

Hike 24: Forbidden Plateau

Hike 26: Crest Mountain

Hike 28: Marble Meadows

Hike 30: Bedwell Lake

Hike 31: Schoen Lake

Hike 33: San Josef Bay/Mount St. Patrick

Hike 41: Clayoquot Valley Witness Trail

Best Hikes for Wildflowers

Hike 7: Mount Tzouhalem

Hike 13: Notch Hill

Hike 14: Englishman River/Morrison Creek

Hike 18: Mount Arrowsmith (Ridge Access Routes)

Hike 19: Mount Arrowsmith (CPR Historic Route)

Hike 20: Della Falls

Hike 21: Alone Mountain

Hike 23: Boston Ridge/Mount Becher

Hike 24: Forbidden Plateau

Hike 26: Crest Mountain

Hike 28: Marble Meadows

Hike 30: Bedwell Lake

Hike 41: Clayoquot Valley Witness Trail

Hike 50: Nootka Island

Best Hikes for Big Trees

Hike 8: Maple Mountain (Blue Trail)

Hike 15: Englishman River/Morrison Creek

Hike 17: Cathedral Grove–MacMillan Provincial Park

Hike 27: Elk River Trail/Landslide Lake

Hike 30: Bedwell Lake

Hike 31: Schoen Lake

Hike 39: Carmanah Valley

Hike 40: Walbran Valley

Hike 41: Clayoquot Valley Witness Trail

Hike 42: Wild Pacific Trail

Hike 44: South Beach Trail

Hike 45: Wickaninnish Trail

Hike 47: Rainforest Figure Eight

Hike 48: Spruce Fringe

Hike 49: Schooner Trail

Hike 50: Nootka Island

Best Hikes for Viewpoints

Hike 5: Mount Finlayson at Goldstream Provincial Park

Hike 7: Mount Tzouhalem

Hike 8: Maple Mountain (Pink and Blue Trails)

Hike 13: Notch Hill

Hike 18: Mount Arrowsmith (Ridge Access Routes)

Hike 19: Mount Arrowsmith (CPR Historic Trail)

Hike 20: Della Falls

Hike 21: Alone Mountain

Hike 23: Boston Ridge/Mount Becher

Hike 24: Forbidden Plateau (Mount Albert Edward)

Hike 26: Crest Mountain

Hike 28: Marble Meadows

Hike 30: Bedwell Lake

Hike 33: San Josef Bay/Mount St. Patrick

Hike 36: Juan de Fuca Marine Trail

Hike 38: West Coast Trail

Best Hikes for Waterfalls

Hike 6: Cowichan River Footpath

Hike 15: Englishman River/Morrison Creek

Hike 16: Little Qualicum Falls Provincial Park

Hike 20: Della Falls

Hike 25: Elk Falls Provincial Park

Hike 27: Elk River Trail/Landslide Lake

Hike 29: Upper Myra Falls

Hike 31: Schoen Lake

Hike 41: Clayoquot Valley Witness Trail

Hike 50: Nootka Island

FURTHER READING

Hiking and Other Adventures

Backroading Vancouver Island, Rosemary Neering, Whitecap Books, 1996.

Hiking the Ancient Forests of British Columbia and Washington, Randy Stoltmann, Lone Pine Publishing, 1996.

Hiking Trails I: Victoria and Vicinity, Susan Lawrence, Vancouver Island Trails Information Society (VITIS), 1997.

Hiking Trails II: South Central Vancouver Island and the Gulf Islands, Richard K. Blier, VITIS, 2000.

Hiking Trails III: Central and Northern Vancouver Island and Quadra Island, James Rutter, VITIS, 1996.

Vancouver Island South Explorer: The Outdoor Guide, Mark Zuehlke, Whitecap Books, 1994.

Island Adventures, Richard K. Blier, Orca Book Publishers, 1989.

Island Backroads: Hiking, Camping and Paddling on Vancouver Island, Richard K. Blier, Orca Book Publishers, 1998.

More Island Adventures, Richard K. Blier, Orca Book Publishers, 1993.

The Backroad Mapbook Volume II: Vancouver Island, Russell and Wesley Mussio, Mussio Ventures Ltd., 2001.

Alberni Valley Trail Guide, the Alberni Environmental Coalition, 1999.

Hiking–Mountain Biking and Adventure Trails, Fred A. C. Rogers, Quadra Printers Ltd., 1994.

Trans Canada Trail: The British Columbia Route, Jason Marleau and Russell Mussio, Mussio Ventures Ltd., 2001.

Field Guides

Exploring the Seashore, Gloria Snively, Gordon Soules Book Publishers Ltd., 1997.

Geology of British Columbia, Sydney G. Cannings, Greystone Books, 1999.

Pacific Coast: National Audobon Nature Guide, Bayard H. and Evelyn McConnaughey, Alfred A. Knopf, 1988.

Plants of Coastal British Columbia, Jim Pojar and Andy MacKinnon, Lone Pine Publishing, 1994.

Sibley Guide to Birds, David Allen Sibley, Alfred A. Knopf, 2000.

Western Birds: An Audubon Handbook, John Farrand Jr., McGraw-Hill Book Company, 1988.

Whelks to Whales: Coastal Marine Life of Oregon, Washington, British Columbia and Alaska, Rick M. Harbo, Harbour Publishing, 2000.

Other Related Books

Barkley Sound: A History of the Pacific Rim National Park Area, Bruce R. Scott, Fleming Review Printing, 1972.

British Columbia: A Natural History, Richard and Sydney Cannings, Greystone Books, 1996.

British Columbia Place Names, G. P. V. and Helen B. Akrigg, Sono Nis Press, 1986.

The Cape Scott Story, Lester R. Petersen, Sunfire, 1985.

Encyclopedia of British Columbia, Daniel Francis, Harbour Book Publishing, 2000.

Genius of Place: Writing About British Columbia, David Stouck and Myler Wilkinson, Polestar Book Publishers, 2000.

How to Shit in the Woods, Kathleen Meyer, Ten Speed Press, 1994.

Nootka Sound and the Surrounding Waters of Maquinna, Heather Harbord, Heritage House, 1996.

Nootka Sound Explored: A West Coast History, Laurie Jones, Ptarmigan Press, 1991.

Provincial and National Park Campgrounds in B.C., Jayne Seagrave, Heritage House, 1997.

Siwiti—A Whale's Story, Alexandra Morton, Orca Book Publishers, 1991.

Strathcona: A History of British Columbia's First Provincial Park, Ptarmigan Press, 1986.

The West Coast Trail and Nitinat Lakes, Douglas and McIntyre, Sierra Club of B.C., 1992.

Where to See Wildlife on Vancouver Island, Kim Goldberg, Harbour Publishing, 1997.

CLUBS AND TRAIL GROUPS

Alberni Valley Outdoor Club: Located in Port Alberni, this group organizes activities including hiking, canoeing, cross-country skiing, and family picnics. Phone (250) 723–9930; Web site www.mountainclubs.bc.ca/clubs/2002sch1. doc; e-mail mford@cedar.alberni.net.

Alpine Club of Canada (Vancouver Island Section): This is a mountaineering club, whose active membership ranges from Victoria to Campbell River. The primary activity is climbing mountains year-round on the Island and in the Coastal Range, Cascades, and Rocky Mountains on foot, skis, or snowshoes. Contact Judith Holm at (250) 477–8596; Web site www.alpineclubofcanada. ca/vi.

B.C. Mountaineering Club: This provincial group organizes activities including hiking, mountaineering, climbing, and ski mountaineering. Phone (604) 268–9502; Web site www.bcmc.ca; e-mail info@bcmc.ca.

Cedar Hill Trail Walkers: This group hosts and organizes a variety of hikes for adults ages fifty and over. Hiking locations include Goldstream Park, East Sooke Park, and Thetis Lake. For more information, call (250) 480–3906.

Comox District Mountaineering Club: CDMC takes part in hiking, mountaineering, cross-country and backcountry skiing, snowshoeing, canoeing, kayaking, and caving activities. Contact Adele Routledge at (604) 336–2130; Web site www.clubtread.com/clubs.asp.

Federation of Mountain Clubs of B.C. and Canada West Mountain School: FMCBC comprises a diverse group of nonmechanized mountain enthusiasts including hikers, mountaineers, backpackers, rock climbers, skiers, snowboarders, and snowshoers with an interest in the protection and preservation of the mountain environment. Phone (604) 878–7007; fax (604) 876–7047; Web site www.mountainclubs.bc.ca; e-mail fmcbc@mountainclubs.bc.ca.

Friends of Ecological Reserves: FER promotes the interests of ecological reserves in British Columbia by raising awareness and funds for research, education, monitoring, maintenance, and field trips. P.O. Box 8477, Station Central, Victoria, BC V8W 3S1; Web site www.ecoreserves.bc.ca; e-mail ecoreserves@hotmail.com.

Greater Victoria Cycling Coalition: Visit the coalition's Victoria storefront to purchase cycling maps, talk to volunteers, browse a library of cycling books and reference material, or learn about cycling in the city. 1056A North Park Street, Victoria, BC V8T 1C6; phone (250) 480–5155; Web site www.gvcc.bc.ca; e-mail gvcc@gvcc.bc.ca.

Morrell Sanctuary Society: This society oversees the workings of the Morrell Nature Sanctuary in Nanaimo. 1050 Nanaimo Lakes Road, Nanaimo, BC V9R 3C2; phone (250) 753–5811; fax (250) 753–8826; Web site morrell.bc.ca; e-mail morrell@nisa.net.

Outdoor Club of Victoria: This group's activities include hiking and skiing mostly in the Greater Victoria area. Phone (250) 920–3893; Web site www.mountainclubs.bc.ca/ocv/.

South Island Mountain Bike Society: SIMBS acts to preserve and increase mountain biking access on Southern Vancouver Island. 215-2680 Quadra Street, Victoria, BC V8T 4E4; phone (250) 477–2455; Web site www.simbs.com; e-mail info@simbs.com.

The Trails Society of British Columbia: The mandate of the Trails Society is to facilitate the development of shared use and sustainable trail networks, including the Trans Canada Trail, within British Columbia. 425-1367 West Broadway, Vancouver, BC V6H 4A9; phone (604) 737–3188; fax (604) 738–7175; Web site www.trailsbc.ca; e-mail trailsbc@trailsbc.ca.

The Trans Canada Trail Foundation: This foundation organizes the business of TCT across Canada. 43 Westminster North, Montreal, Quebec H4X 1Y8; toll free (888) 465–3636; Web site www.tctrail.ca; e-mail info@tctrail.ca.

Vancouver Island Trails Information Society: This Victoria-based group publishes the series *Hiking Trails I, II, and III* sold at Island bookstores. Web site www.mountainclubs.bc.ca/voa; e-mail trails@hikingtrailbooks.com.

Victoria Club Tread: Members receive a newsletter in the mail and participate in members-only events. Nonmembers must try three outdoor events before applying for membership. Web site www.clubtread.org; e-mail Pat Brown at accord@pacificcoastnet.

Wild Pacific Trail Society: The Wild Pacific Trail Society is a registered non-profit organization. All monies received by the society are allocated toward trail enhancement, promotion, and further development of the Wild Pacific Trail. Box 48, Ucluelet, BC V0R 3A0; Web site www.longbeachmaps.com/wildtrail.html; e-mail wildpacifictrail@hotmail.com.

ABOUT THE AUTHORS

Shannon Cowan

Lissa Cowan

Sisters Shannon and Lissa Cowan moved to Vancouver Island to explore a quieter lifestyle and pursue outdoor opportunities. Now living and working in the mid-island area, Shannon is a novelist and freelance writer and Lissa is a writer, translator, and senior communications coordinator. While Shannon has published her first novel, *Leaving Winter* (Oolichan Books, 2000), and written for Canadian and U.S. periodicals, Lissa has written for Canadian newspapers and periodicals, published translations from French, and written about Pacific forests. Both have explored the far reaches of Vancouver Island on foot, bicycle, kayak, and canoe and share an enthusiastic interest in protecting the pristine areas of their island home.